Cohousing

A Contemporary Approach to Housing Ourselves

Kathryn McCamant and Charles Durrett

H A B I T A T   P R E S S   /   T E N   S P E E D   P R E S S

Berkeley, California

Dedicated to
Jan Gudmand-Høyer
who with vision,
endurance, and above
all, faith in his fellow
citizens, played a
critical role in the
development of
cohousing communities.

Acknowledgements

For helping to make this book possible, we would like to thank the hundreds of people in cohousing communities with whom we talked, shared afternoon tea, ate dinner, and became especially well acquainted over late-night glasses of wine when some of our best research was accomplished. For their hospitality, we would like to give special thanks to the cohousing communities of Trudeslund and Skråplanet.

We would also like to thank the Academy of Art and Architecture in Copenhagen (particularly Jørgen Peder Hansen), Erik Skoven of the Danish International Studies Program, Jan W. Hansen of the Architecture School in Aarhus, and the Danish Building Research Institute (particularly Hans S. Andersen and Erik Jantzen).

Stateside there is no end to the list of people to whom we owe the sincerest gratitude for their help and support. For editorial, layout, and typing assistance, Janet Guastavino, Mario and Sara Guttman, Susanna Kohn, Julie Levetzoe, Frank Livingston, Constance McKnight, Robin Mitchell (and Tom who walked in looking for Robin and stayed for two days of proofreading), and Francoise Pereira. For translating, thanks go to Erik Fehmerling, Ling Larsen, and Hans Rasmusen; for drawing assistance, Kurt Gettmen, Peter Waller, Bruce Fukuji, and even the reluctant but reliable Chris Ramm; for encouragement and support, our families, Ann Howell, Dan Gonzales, and Judy Steiner, and for their patience, our housemates, Marc and Yari. For general assistance at every stage and moral support far beyond the call of duty we'd especially like to thank Charlie Huizenga, Charmaine Curtis, and Joshua Simon who made sure we still danced on occasion, if not enough.

Research for this book was partially funded by the Ib Henriksens Fond, the February 3rd Fond, the Kreditforeningen Danmarks Fond, and the Byggeriets Realkredit Fond.

Edited by Kathleen Goss
Copy edit by Susan Chun
Book design by Yari Jeada

Cohousing is a trademark of McCamant & Durrett. All rights reserved. Contact McCamant & Durrett through the publisher for permission to use the term.

Library of Congress Cataloging-in-Publication Data
McCamant, Kathryn M., 1959–
    Cohousing: a contemporary approach to housing ourselves.

    Bibliography: p.
    Includes index.
    1. Housing, Cooperative—Denmark. 2. Housing, Cooperative—United States. I. Durrett, Charles R., 1955–   . II. Title.
HD7287.72.D4M37 1988   334.1'09489   88-80988

ISBN 0-89815-306-9

TEN SPEED PRESS
PO Box 7123
Berkeley, California 94707

Printed in the United States of America

2 3 4 5 6 — 93 92 91 90 89

TABLE OF CONTENTS

PREFACE

This book is about places which expand the meanings of "home," "neighborhood," and "community." We wrote it to share the inspiration we found in these places with others who have also dreamed of a home that not only provides shelter, but is also part of a community. We hope that this book will inspire people to take a more active role in creating the home and neighborhood they want to live in.

Adaptations of the cohousing concept to other cultures are likely to reflect different priorities. Nevertheless, the two decades of undeniably successful experience of Danish cohousing provides a wealth of information we can learn from. The Danes have long been recognized as leaders in design and housing, and especially in appreciating the social impact of the physical environment. Their standard of living is one of the highest in the world. With Denmark's history of prosperity and innovation, we can begin to understand why cohousing was pioneered there. Unfortunately, until now, virtually no information on cohousing was available in English.

The book is organized in three parts. Part One introduces the concept —what it is like to live in such a place. Part Two takes a closer look at eight communities which illustrate the diversity of cohousing possibilities. Part Three examines cohousing's evolution, the mechanics of developing cohousing, and specific design considerations. It concludes with a discussion of how the concept is being applied in the United States—what are the potential obstacles, and what development strategies are appropriate.

We hope these examples will inspire you as much as they inspired us. We can now go on to build on the Danish experience, and we promise that the next edition of this book will include new cohousing communities built in the United States. Will you be living in one? We will!

FOREWORD

Housing, private and public, across the developed and developing world is everywhere pretty much the same, and pretty terrible. It seems set up to crowd together unrelated and hermetic nuclear families whose only link with each other is that they have been brought together by some mindless central casting to play bit parts in an incomprehensible urban drama. As much attention is devoted to ensuring privacy as money will allow, with no attention to providing for community, ever. The format is particularly inappropriate since the family unit apparently served—father who works, mother who takes care of the children (1.6 or 2.2 or however many the country supposedly averages) —seldom exists either among the extended families found in some parts of the world or in the variety of living arrangements found in the United States.

Into all these unsuitable arrangements this book comes like a breath of fresh air. The authors look insightfully at places (it turns out there are some) where people have chosen to provide for community as well as privacy, where adults and children value each other, and remain interested in concerns beyond themselves.

The authors have looked carefully at the physical arrangements of community housing and those settings that support new ways of living. *Cohousing* rings true—it is interesting, well balanced, and without hype. In short, this is a reasonable and even frequently fascinating account of a topic presently of small dimensions, but of enormous importance for the future of housing, and of us all.

Charles W. Moore, Architect

PART ONE

Introducing Cohousing

*T*raditional forms of housing no longer address the needs of many people. Dramatic demographic and economic changes are taking place in our society and most of us feel the effects of these trends in our own lives. Things that people once took for granted—family, community, a sense of belonging—must now be actively sought out. Many people are mis-housed, ill-housed or unhoused because of the lack of appropriate options. These chapters introduce a new housing model which addresses such changes. Pioneered primarily in Denmark and now being adapted in other countries, the cohousing concept reestablishes many of the advantages of traditional villages within the context of late twentieth-century life.

CHAPTER ONE

Addressing Our Changing Lifestyles

everal years ago, as a young married couple, we began to think about where we were going to raise our children. What kind of setting would allow us to best combine our professional careers with child rearing? Already our lives were hectic. Often we would come home from work exhausted and hungry, only to find the refrigerator empty. Between our jobs and housekeeping, where would we find the time to spend with our kids? Relatives lived in distant cities, and even our friends lived across town. Just to get together for coffee we had to make arrangements two weeks in advance. Most young parents we knew seemed to spend most of their time shuttling their children to and from day care and playmates' homes, leaving little opportunity for anything else.

After work, I pick up groceries while my husband picks up the kids from day care. Once we get home, we cook dinner, clean up, and put the kids to bed. We don't have time for each other, let alone anyone else. There's got to be a better way.

Working mother

So many of us seemed to be living in places that did not accommodate our most basic needs; we always had to drive somewhere to do anything sociable. Even if we saw a house we could afford, we didn't really want to buy it. We dreamed of a better solution—an affordable neighborhood where children would have playmates and we would have friends nearby; a place with people of all ages, young and old, where neighbors knew and helped each other.

Professionally, we had both designed different types of housing. We had been amazed at the conservatism of most architects and housing professionals, and at the lack of consideration given to people's changing needs. Single-family houses, apartments, and condominiums might change in price and occasionally in style, but otherwise they were designed to function pretty much as they had for the last 40 years. Perhaps our own frustrations were indicative of a larger problem, a diverse population attempting to fit itself into housing types that are simply no longer appropriate for many people.

Contemporary postindustrial societies such as the United States and Western Europe are undergoing a multitude of changes that affect our housing needs. The modern single-family detached home, which makes up 67 percent of the American housing stock, was designed for a nuclear family consisting of a breadwinning father, a homemaking mother, and two to four children. Today, less than one-quarter of the United States population lives in such households. Rather, the family with two working parents predominates, while the single-parent household is the fastest-growing family type. Almost one-quarter of the population lives alone, and this proportion is predicted to grow as the number of Americans over the age of 60 increases. At the same time, the surge in housing costs and the increasing mobility of the population combine to break

down traditional community ties and place more demands on individual households. These factors call for a thorough reexamination of household and community needs, and the way we house ourselves.

A Danish Solution

As we searched for more desirable living situations, we kept thinking about the new developments we had visited while studying architecture in Denmark several years earlier. After numerous futile efforts to obtain information in English about what the Danes were doing, we decided to go and find out for ourselves. This book is about what we found.

In Denmark, people frustrated by the available housing options have developed a new housing type that redefines the concept of neighborhood to fit contemporary lifestyles. Tired of the isolation and impracticalities of single-family houses and apartment units, they have built housing that combines the autonomy of private dwellings with the advantages of community living. Each household has a private residence, but also shares extensive common facilities with the larger group, such as a kitchen and dining hall, children's playrooms, workshops, guest rooms, and laundry facilities. Although individual dwellings are designed to be self-sufficient and each has its own kitchen, the common facilities, and particularly common dinners, are an important aspect of community life both for social and practical reasons.

By the fall of 1989, more than 120 of these communities had been built in Denmark with many more planned. They range in size from 6 to 80 households, with the majority between 15 and 33 residences. These communities are called *bofællesskaber* in Danish (directly translated as "living communities"), for which we have coined the English term "cohousing." First built in the early 1970s, cohousing developments have quadrupled in

Residents relax before dinner on the terrace in front of the common house.

number in the last five years. Their success and growing acceptance attests to the viability of the concept.

Imagine . . .

It's five o'clock in the evening, and Anne is glad the work day is over. As she pulls into her driveway, she begins to unwind at last. Some neighborhood kids dart through the trees, playing a mysterious game at the edge of the gravel parking lot. Her daughter yells, "Hi Mom!" as she runs by with three other children.

Instead of frantically trying to put together a nutritious dinner, Anne can relax now, spend some time with her children, and then eat with her family in the common house. Walking through the common house on her way home, she stops to chat with the evening's cooks, two of her neighbors, who are busy preparing dinner—broiled chicken with mushroom sauce—in the kitchen. Several children are setting the tables. Outside on the patio, some neighbors share a pot of tea in the late afternoon sun. Anne waves hello, and continues down the lane to her own house, catching glimpses into the kitchens of the houses she passes. Here a child is seated, doing homework at the kitchen table; next door, John reads his ritual after-work newspaper.

After dropping off her things at home,

A child sets the table for dinner in the common house.

Anne walks through the birch trees behind the houses to the child-care center where she picks up her four-year-old son, Peter. She will have some time to read Peter a story before dinner, she thinks to herself.

Anne and her husband, Eric, live with their two children in a housing development that they helped design. Not that either of them is an architect or builder: Anne works at the county administration office, and Eric is an engineer. Six years ago they joined a group of families who were looking for a realistic housing alternative. At that time, they owned their own home, had a three-year-old daughter, and were contemplating having another child—partly so that their daughter would have a playmate in their predominantly adult neighborhood. One day they noticed a short announcement in the local newspaper:

Most housing options available today isolate the family and discourage a neighborhood atmosphere. Alternatives are needed. If you are interested in

- living in a large, social community,

- having your own house,

- and participating in the planning of your home,

perhaps this is for you. We, a group of 20 families, are planning a housing development which addresses our needs both for community and private life. If this interests you, call about our next meeting.

Anne and Eric attended the meeting, where they found other people who expressed similar frustrations about their existing housing situations. The group's goal was to build a housing development with a lively and positive social environment. They wanted a place where children would live near playmates; where individuals would

have a feeling of belonging; where they would know people of all ages; and where they would be able to grow old and continue to contribute productively.

In the months that followed, the group further defined their goals and began the long, difficult process of turning their dream into reality. Some people dropped out and others joined. Two and a half years later, Anne and Eric moved into their new home—a community of clustered houses that share a large common house. By working together, these people had created the kind of neighborhood they wanted to live in, a cohousing community.

Today Tina, Anne and Eric's eight-year-old daughter, never lacks for playmates. She remembers their old house with its big backyard. It was a great place for playing make-believe games, but she had to play by herself most of the time. Tina liked to visit the nice old man who lived at the end of the street, but Mom wouldn't let her leave their yard by herself, worrying that "something might happen and I wouldn't know."

Residents stop and chat as they come and go during the day.

Now Tina walks home from school with the other kids in the community. Her mother is usually at work, so Tina goes up to the common house, where one of the adults makes tea and toast for the kids and any other adults who are around. She likes talking with the adults, especially Peter, who tells great stories. If it is raining, Tina and her friends play in the kids' room, where they can make plenty of noise if they want. Other days, when Tina has homework or just feels like being alone, she goes home after tea time, or she may visit an older girl who lives three houses down from her. Tina liked her family's old house, but this place is much more interesting. There's so much to do; she can play outside all day, and, as long as she doesn't leave the community, her mother doesn't worry about her.

John and Karen moved into the same community a few years after it was built. Their kids were grown and had left home. Now they enjoy the peacefulness of having a house to themselves; they have time to take classes in the evenings, visit art museums, and attend an occasional play in town. John teaches children with learning disabilities, and plans to retire in a few years. Karen administers a senior citizens' housing complex and nursing home. They lead full and active lives, but worry about getting older. How long will their health hold out? Will one die, leaving the other alone? Such considerations, combined with the desire to be part of an active community while maintaining their independence, led John and Karen to buy a one-bedroom home in this community. Here they feel secure knowing their neighbors

Living in cohousing is like living with an extended family—the children have playmates of all ages. Here the older children have built a swimming pool for the younger ones.

care about them. If John gets sick, people will be there to help Karen with the groceries or join her at the theater. Common dinners relieve them of preparing a meal every night, and their children and grandchildren can stay in the community's guest rooms when they visit. They are part of a diverse community with children and adults of all ages. John and Karen enjoy a house without children, but it's still refreshing to see kids playing outside, or to share with them the excitement of finding a special flower in the garden.

A New Housing Type

For Anne, Eric, Tina, John, and Karen, cohousing provides the community support that they missed in their previous homes. Cohousing is a grass-roots movement that grew directly out of people's dissatisfaction

with existing housing choices. Its initiators draw inspiration from the increasing popularity of shared households, in which several unrelated people share a traditional house, and from the cooperative movement in general. Yet cohousing is distinctive in that each family or household has a separate dwelling and chooses how much they want to participate in community activities. Other innovative ideas are also being experimented with—single-parent cooperatives and congregate housing for the elderly with private rooms arranged around shared living spaces. But unlike these other approaches, cohousing developments are not targeted for any specific age or family type; residents represent a cross section of old and young, families and singles.

Cohousing also differs from most of the intentional communities and communes we

A couple enjoys a quiet moment on their back patio.

know in the United States, which are often organized around strong ideological beliefs and may depend on a charismatic leader to establish the direction of the community and hold the group together. Most intentional communities function as educational or spiritual centers. Cohousing, on the other hand, offers a new approach to housing rather than a new way of life. Based on democratic principles, cohousing developments espouse no ideology other than the desire for a more practical and social home environment.

Cohousing communities are unique in their extensive common facilities, and more importantly, in that they are organized, planned, and managed by the residents themselves. The great variety in their size, ownership structure, and design illustrates the many diverse applications of this concept.

The first cohousing development was built in 1972 outside Copenhagen, Denmark, by 27 families who wanted a greater sense of community than was available in suburban subdivisions or apartment complexes. They desired a neighborhood with a child-friendly environment and the opportunity for cooperation in daily household functions like laundry, meals, and child care. Today, cohousing has become an accepted housing option in Denmark, with new projects being planned and built in ever increasing numbers.

Although the concept was pioneered in Denmark and the largest number of cohousing developments are located there, people in other countries are beginning to build their own variations. In the Netherlands especially, more and more people are finding that cohousing addresses their needs better than other existing choices. More than thirty such housing developments have been built in the Netherlands, with nearly as many planned. Architects, planners, and government officials from Sweden, Norway, Germany, and as far away as Japan and Nigeria have visited the cohousing developments in Denmark and the Netherlands, and similar communities are now being built in Sweden, Norway, France, and Germany. We have chosen to focus on cohousing in Denmark because of the depth and diversity of their experience, and because we believe the Danish experience is the most applicable to the American context.

Our Field Work
In 1984 and 1985 we spent 13 months visiting 46 cohousing communities in Denmark, the Netherlands, and Sweden. Many of these communities served as our home for periods of several days to six months. We talked with residents, architects, planners, builders, lawyers, and bankers. We also worked with the Danish Building Research Institute and the Royal Academy of Art and Architecture in Copenhagen. But the most valuable part of our work was living in cohousing and experiencing day-to-day life through different seasons and personal moods. We ate most of our dinners in the common houses, and took our turns cooking just as the other residents did. People shared with us many of their profoundest insights during late-night conversations over a bottle of wine.

We found these communities immensely inspiring. From the moment we entered any one of them, it was apparent that we were in a special place. Residents took great pride in what they had created through their cooperative efforts. Yet, they were also aware of the community's shortcomings, and freely discussed all aspects of building and living in this type of housing.

Our evaluation of cohousing focused on its ability to create a positive and humane environment, as evidenced by the feelings of those who live there, the experiences of those who have left, and our own observations and comparisons of the different developments. While we found the most innova-

tive, trend-setting developments very exciting, the many more ordinary examples
demonstrated the broad acceptance of the
cohousing idea.

A home is more than a roof over one's
head or a financial investment. It can provide
a sense of security and comfort, or elicit feelings of frustration, loneliness, or fear. The
home environment affects a person's confidence, relationships with others, and personal satisfaction. A woman who worries at
work about when she will shop for groceries
and get dinner on the table is often unable
to concentrate on her job or relax with her
children once she is home, let alone take
time for herself. This aspect of housing cannot be measured by cost, internal rates of
return, or other traditional methods of real
estate assessment. While this book does discuss financing methods and market values,
our most important concern is people themselves and the quality of their lives.

*Dinner time at Trudeslund's
common house.*

CHAPTER TWO

I know I live in a community because on a Friday night it takes me 45 minutes and two beers to get from the parking lot to my front door.

Trudeslund resident

How Cohousing Works:
The Trudeslund Community

People drift into the common house. The few minutes before dinner are a time to relax and catch up on each other's lives. At one of the tables, a little girl tells her parents about her day at preschool. Shrieks of laughter come from the playroom down the hall. The cooks put the last touches on the salad. By six o'clock the dining hall is bustling with life as people find their seats. It's dinner time at Trudeslund.

For the 33 families who live in the cohousing community of Trudeslund, this was a typical evening. For us, it was the first of many such evenings we would spend in the Trudeslund common house. We were not certain that first night how we would adjust to eating regularly with 50 or more people, but our wariness was soon dispelled. After experiencing the convenience and pleasantness of common dinners and community life as a whole, we wondered why we had ever considered living any other way.

Dinner is served in the common house every night (except for two Saturdays a month when the room is used for private parties). Each of the private houses also has a full kitchen, so that residents may participate in common dinners as often as they like. Many residents eat in the common house three or four times a week, and have more intimate family dinners at home the other evenings. Some eat almost every night in the common house, using the time they save from shopping, cooking, and cleaning up to spend with their children. We quickly came to appreciate having several extra hours each day. Community dinners are not only convenient, but also pleasant social gatherings filled with interesting conversation. On any given evening, 50 percent of the residents, and often more, take part.

The one responsibility required of every adult resident is to cook dinner. Two adults, assisted by one child, plan, shop, prepare, serve, and wash up after dinner. Cooking for 60 may seem like an enormous job for two people, but with a well-equipped community kitchen, it's not much more complicated than cooking for six in a normal kitchen

Residents rotate responsibility for preparing common dinners so that two adults cook each evening.

—you just learn to use ten times as much of everything. Residents sign up for dinners at least two days in advance and pay for the meal after dinner, when the cooks have divided the cost by the number eating—typically about $1 to $1.50 for adults, half price for children under thirteen, and free for toddlers under three.

The first time we prepared a common dinner—enchiladas for 80—was an intimidating experience. But the satisfaction we felt at the end of the evening made up for all our anxieties. Our next efforts were considerably easier as we learned the ropes of cooking for large groups. One resident, a doctor, told us he had been very apprehensive about cooking for the community; he had never really cooked for himself, let alone for 50 people. To his surprise, he had not only succeeded, but discovered he actually enjoyed cooking and began to cook more at home as well. With more than 60 adults in the community, each has to cook only once a month. Cooking one day a month is well worth the time and trouble when you can just show up for dinner the other 29 days. Trudeslund residents are convinced that they have the best dinner system of all—it's dependable, yet flexible enough to accommodate the changing needs of each family. We have to agree.

The Place

As our primary base and home for six months, Trudeslund is the cohousing community we know best. Situated in the town of Birkerød, just north of Copenhagen, its 33 residences and large common house were completed in the spring of 1981. Utilizing the natural features of the sloping, wooded site, the residences line two pedestrian streets, with the common house located at the highest point where the streets meet. With cars kept at the edge of the site and the houses clustered together, much of the lower

Trudeslund's common house.

Although their community was built at the same density as single-family houses in the area (upper right), Trudeslund residents chose to cluster the 33 dwellings along two pedestrian streets, localize parking, and preserve the wooded portion of the site.

21

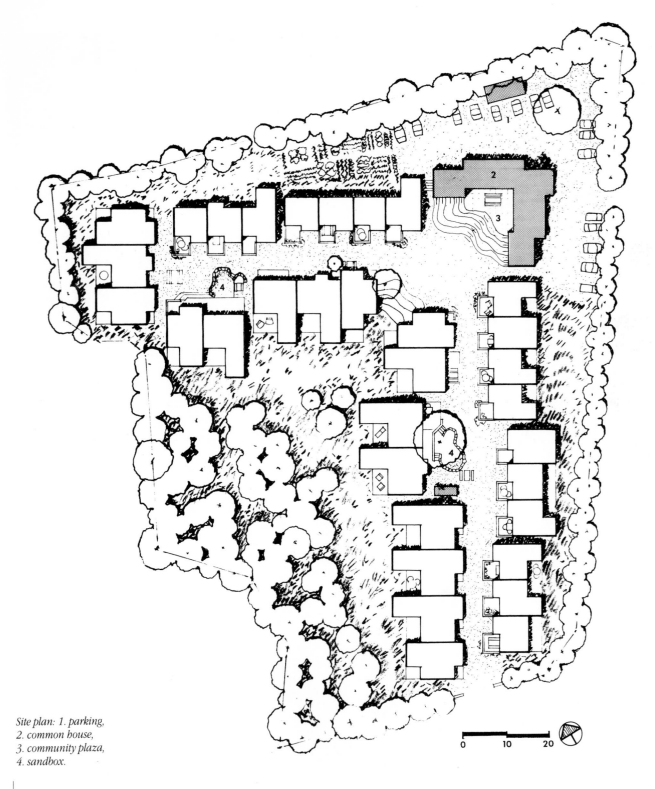

Site plan: 1. parking,
2. common house,
3. community plaza,
4. sandbox.

Row houses with small front gardens line the pedestrian streets where much of the community's socializing takes place. The play areas are primary gathering spots for both children and adults.

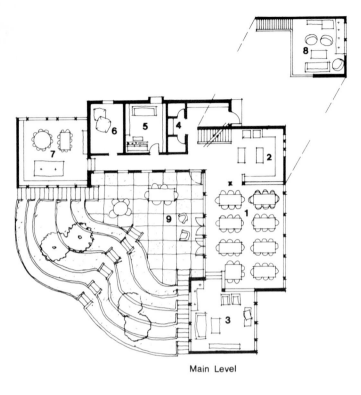

Main Level

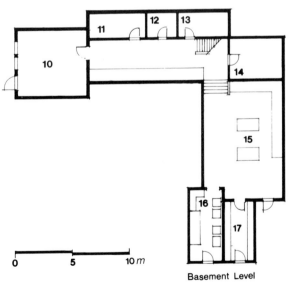

Basement Level

0   5   10 m

Common house floor plans: 1. dining room, 2. kitchen, 3. TV room, 4. bathrooms, 5. guest room, 6. children's pillow room, 7. children's room, 8. library, 9. terrace, 10. teen room, 11. storage, 12. photography darkroom, 13. freezer, 14. furnace, 15. workshop, 16. laundry, 17. store.

The workshop.

The teenagers' music room.

In the common house residents never have to watch the game alone.

end is left wooded, making it a favorite place for children to play. Architecturally, socially, and practically, this community has succeeded in creating a very "livable" environment.

Shared Resources

Common dinners are only one of the practical advantages of living in Trudeslund. A cooperative store, located in the common house, is stocked with household goods, from toothpaste to cornflakes. Each household has a key, so that residents can pick up goods at any hour. They write down what they take in the account book and receive a bill at the end of the month. We wondered if goods ever disappeared without being noted in the account book. Indeed, there are occasional discrepancies (probably because people forget to write items down, rather than purposely steal), which must be made up from the community budget. Residents know that serious problems with the accounts would cause the store to be closed.

The store is run by one of nine "interest groups." Every adult is a member of one such group. Other interest groups are responsible for the outdoor areas, special children's activities, the monthly newsletter and minutes of meetings, the heating system, the laundry room, general maintenance, social events, and overall coordination of community activities.

Two washing machines and one dryer accommodate the laundry needs of the more than one hundred residents. If both machines are full, clothes baskets are left in line with washing instructions. When residents take their laundry out, they put in the next load in line, so no one has to wait for an empty machine. Detergent is bought in bulk as part of the common budget. While all the houses were designed to accommodate a washer and dryer, only one family has chosen to install its own.

Also located in the common house are a workshop, a darkroom for photography, a television room, a walk-in freezer used by the community store and individual families, a guest room, and a music room where teenagers can "jam" on drums and electric guitars without bothering anyone. A recent addition is the computer. A study the government is conducting on different possibilities for working at home has provided every household in Trudeslund with a personal computer connected to a central computer in the common house and outside computer lines. Twenty-nine of the households have also pooled their resources to buy a 17-room vacation house in Sweden.

These facilities are only a small part of Trudeslund's practical advantages. In such a community it's easy to borrow occasional necessities or share ownership. For instance, two families share a car, while five others own a sailboat together. There is only one lawn mower. Items needed only occasionally, such as tools, typewriters, and camping equipment, can generally be borrowed or shared, instead of each family owning one of everything. This sharing of resources gives all residents access to a wider variety of conveniences at a lower cost per family than is possible in traditional single-family houses.

Advantages for Children

With nearly fifty children living in Trudeslund, there is no lack of playmates. The pedestrian-oriented site gives them lots of room to run without worrying about cars. The community serves as a large, extended family—children have many people besides their parents to look after them, to whom they can turn for assistance, or just to talk to. It becomes second nature for the older kids to keep an eye on the smaller ones, and the adults know every child by name.

Child care is still needed during the daytime, when most of the parents are at work.

After considering many possibilities, including local public facilities, the community decided to start their own after-school program and to send preschoolers to existing child-care centers in the neighborhood.

Initially, a "child-care corps" of five to seven adults rotated responsibility for 12 to 15 youngsters from noon to early evening when their parents came home. Other adults were also expected to help out at least five days a year. During the first two years, this system was adjusted several times, becoming more and more loosely structured until it dissolved almost completely. Because the children had grown older and were more familiar with the community and each other, they no longer required such structured care. Many adults also found that a forty-hour-a-week job simply did not permit them the

extra time to run a child-care program.

Today, the younger children attend a publicly run preschool and kindergarten which has been opened in an old cottage adjacent to the community. Because of its proximity and its special relationship to the residents of Trudeslund, who were instrumental in establishing it, this school is almost a part of the community. After school, older children may hang out in the common house, play outside, or go home. The evening's cooks are usually working in the community kitchen and other adults are available if a child needs assistance.

Afternoon tea, a vestige of the community day-care program, provides a meeting place for both children and adults. Every afternoon at three o'clock tea is served in the common house. Although officially an activity for the

The children at Trudeslund never lack for playmates or baby sitters.

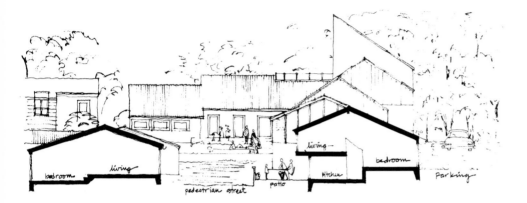

A section through the site shows the relationship between private, semiprivate, and common areas.

kids, adults also enjoy afternoon tea. On the days we were working at home, we always looked forward to tea time, the cohousing equivalent of the office coffee break.

Baby sitters are never lacking in the community. One couple, needing some time alone, went away for several days, leaving their sons, ages two and seven, with neighbors. The boys were quite comfortable staying with their neighbors and the parents knew they need not worry. As we watched the Trudeslund kids playing after dinner—their interaction with each other and with adults, their self-confidence, and their ability to articulate their thoughts—we could truly appreciate the benefits that children derive from a sense of community.

A Social Atmosphere

The obvious practical advantages—child care, common dinners, shared resources—are not the main reasons why people choose to live in Trudeslund. One resident, John Nielsen, wrote:

Our primary motive for wanting to live in a community was the desire for a richer social atmosphere—for both children and adults. The many practical advantages which we later discovered, we hadn't even thought of in the beginning.[1]

One of the objectives stated by Trudeslund's initiators in the development program was to create a social network that would provide more support for the nuclear family:

We want to open the family up toward the community, but still have it [the family] *as a base. We want to have the necessary daily functions in the private dwellings, but transfer as many as possible of the other functions to the community, thereby encouraging social interaction.*

The rich social atmosphere at Trudeslund is most evident on a warm day along the walkways between houses. Here children play, people relax with a beer after work, and families enjoy leisurely Saturday morning breakfasts. All the dwellings have private patios in back, but people seem to prefer sitting in front along the main circulation paths, where they can visit with neighbors or just watch the activity.

The community's design encourages social interaction by providing small courtyards along the walkways, complete with sandboxes and picnic tables, and patios and garden areas directly outside each house, with visual access from the houses themselves. Neighbors tend to congregate around

27

the picnic tables and sandboxes where they can watch the children play. People sit on their front patios whenever weather permits, enjoying the comfortable vantage point just outside their front doors.

In the houses, the kitchen-dining area —the room most families "live" in—looks onto the street, allowing parents to watch children playing outside, or to ask a passing neighbor about a recipe. As John Nielsen describes it:

> In Trudeslund we don't draw the curtains, so one can look in and glimpse life in the different houses. But from the front room [the kitchen-dining area] one also feels part of what happens on the street. Perhaps some would call it nosiness, I call it openness and sharing life.[2]

Each house also has a living area away from the street, which affords complete pri-

vacy. The sensitive relationship between the community area and private dwelling allows for many kinds of socializing. In fact, contrary to many outsiders' apprehensions, we never heard a resident complain about lack of privacy. Living in a close community, people learn to respect each other's occasional need to be unsociable.

Building a Dream

Looking at Trudeslund today, it is easy to forget the difficult process necessary to transform the initial ideas into reality. In December 1978, 20 families formed a group to build a cohousing development on a site available for sale, but zoned for single-family houses. At that time, only eight cohousing communities had been built in Denmark, though many were in the planning process. Under pressure to submit a project proposal quickly to secure the site, members of the group did not have sufficient time to clarify

Residents enjoy Saturday afternoon tea along the pedestrian lane.

their objectives. Only after a dramatic division that caused half of the original members to drop out, followed by a cautious restructuring of goals, was the group able to formulate a development program.

With their goals and objectives agreed upon and the development program formulated, the group held a limited architectural competition, inviting four firms to submit design proposals. After much debate, Vandkunsten Architects, a young, innovative firm, was selected to design and supervise construction of the development.

The two and a half years from the first planning meetings to the completion of construction were hectic and often frustrating. The group's commitment to making all decisions democratically meant numerous long meetings. Two participants later wrote:

We had a flood of work groups going —many meetings in small groups where problems were discussed, and community decision meetings with two-foot-long agendas. Everyone was involved in the work. In the most active period there was at least one meeting a week for the least involved, and three or four for the most involved, after which came "homework" to prepare for the next meetings.[3]

Economic pressures, especially climbing interest rates, disciplined the group's ambitions and kept them to a tight time schedule.

To this day, the architects remember the process of working with the Trudeslund group as very exasperating. According to project architect Michael Sten Johnsen:

Here we have a group of people who are used to being treated individually by virtue of their education, income, and influence; that they wished to act as a community was a dilemma throughout the project.[4]

Residents in charge of the community store meet once a month to discuss business and individual responsibilities.

Many of the participants were well-educated professionals who had strong opinions on the planning and development of the project, but few had previous experience with group decision making. Although the project is regarded as a success by the residents and has been widely publicized, the architects feel they failed to realize their architectural ideals because of the compromises made during the design process. The architects wanted to push cooperative concepts further than the residents were willing to go. They advocated even smaller houses to reduce costs and promote the use of community areas. Residents, most of whom had growing families, were already taking financial risks and did not want homes so unconventional that they would have difficulty selling them. Conflicts between client and architect are common, but the participatory nature of this project, where strong-willed architects confronted equally strong-willed residents, made for a fiery design process.

Still, most residents involved in the planning process agree that their participation was vital to the project's success. Not only did their involvement result in a design that

fit their specific needs and desires, but it helped to define the group's ideals and to strengthen community spirit: "We learned each other's strong and weak sides, and to be open with each other."[5]

In retrospect, residents acknowledge that they would have done some things differently. Many feel they overemphasized the design of the individual houses in relation to the common areas. One participant explained:

> *It's difficult to imagine what you want in a common house because you've never had anything like it before. But everyone knows what they want in their own kitchen.*

Although the group attempted to restrict the floor plans to four basic designs, individual preferences—particularly with regard to

Each dwelling has a private back patio but residents have found no need for fences.

A private residence.

The sanctity of the private dwelling remains well respected.

the kitchens—resulted in 33 variations. Today, most residents agree that standardized kitchens would have been fine, since they eat dinner so often in the common house. Standardization would have reduced construction costs—a lesson from which more recent communities have benefited.

The houses, although not luxurious, are quite comfortable. Ranging in size from 970 to 1,500 square feet (90 to 140 square meters; m²)⁶, they feature vaulted ceilings and wood floors. The one-story houses on the lower, southern side of the pedestrian street allow the two-story houses on the north side to enjoy sun and views of the trees. Unfortunately, the attractive interior design does not make up for the lack of sound insulation between rooms; from any room, a person can easily hear what's going on in the rest of the house.

The houses are privately owned, using a financial structure similar to that of American condominiums, where each resident owns a house and a portion of the common areas. Cohousing is generally more affordable than single-family houses, but Trudeslund's location and the time it was built make it one of the more expensive developments. Situated on valuable property near the train station with a direct line into central Copenhagen, Trudeslund is also close to a forested recreation area, lakes, and the pleasant town of Birkerød. The cost was further increased by 1980–81 interest rates, which had reached an all-time high of 21 percent. Upon completion, the price of a house and a share of the common facilities ranged from 777,000 to 1,000,000 Danish Kroner (DKr) (approximately $91,400 to $117,600).⁷ These figures are comparable to single-family residences in the surrounding area that have no common facilities.

Section through House Two

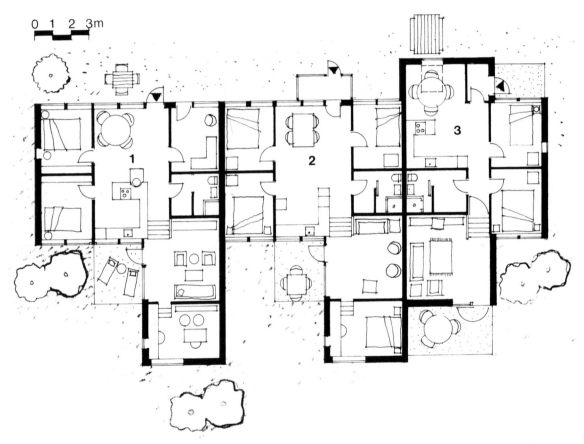

Floor plans of three adjacent dwellings. 1. Four-bedroom unit; direct access to front bedroom makes it ideal for a home office, 1,185 ft² (110 m²). 2. Four-bedroom unit with green house entrance. 3. Two-bedroom unit, 970 ft² (90 m²).

Houses in Trudeslund have sold quickly and their resale value has steadily climbed. While a developer might consider this a measure of success, the residents find it disconcerting that their community is moving further out of the economic grasp of many people. Because the houses are privately owned and no limitations on profits were written into the initial contracts, there is little the group can do to control resale prices.

The ability to make monthly house payments is the only formal determinant for who lives at Trudeslund. For most households, this means two incomes are necessary. Whereas other communities have built smaller units to accommodate single-income households, at Trudeslund single-income households often rent out a room in order to make ends meet.

Residents contend that other living

expenses are less for families at Trudeslund than for households living alone. A resident explained:

Although our monthly house payment increased, our total lifestyle costs decreased because of the common facilities and shared resources available here. Common dinners in particular have cut down the amount we spend on food and the frequency with which we eat out.

Despite the issue of affordability, the residents are quite a diverse group. Adults range in age from 28 to 67. There are four households with no children, nine single parents (seven of whom are fathers), and several singles. Professionally, they include thirteen engineers and computer programmers, eleven elementary and secondary school teachers, four doctors, three economists, two dentists, two nurses, a journalist, and a manager of a chain of radio equipment stores. Fluctuating from year to year, there may be a few full-time parents, someone going back to school or temporarily unemployed, and soon, a few retirees.

At first we feared that with such an interesting group of residents and so many community activities, residents might feel little need to participate in the surrounding neighborhood. Quite the contrary, Trudeslund residents are active in the local theater, politics, schools, and sports teams. The common house is often used for meetings, including practice for the local samba band. Through Trudeslund's social network, residents become aware of neighborhood activities they may have never known about before.

The residents of Trudeslund readily admit they have not built a utopia; that was not their intention. Old problems remain unresolved and new ones have appeared. There are long, frustrating meetings, compromises and disagreements over what needs to be

done and how to do it. Some residents, dissatisfied with the level of community participation, point out how many hours the common house sits empty. Yet the residents of Trudeslund have built a special place, whose unique qualities can be observed every night in the common house when the children are playing and the adults sip their coffee, talking long after dinner is finished.

Notes

1. John Nielsen wrote a postscript ("Efterskrift") for *Veje til Bofaellesskab* in November 1982, a year and a half after moving into Trudeslund (Byggeriets Udviklingsråd, 1983), 136.
2. Ibid., 138.
3. H. S. Andersen and John Nielsen, "Okonomisk risiko og hardt arbejde ved bofaellesskabs projekt," *Blød By 13* (1981): 22–23.
4. Michael Sten Johnsen, "Apropos Trudeslund," *Arkitektur 6* (1982): 248.
5. Nielsen, *Veje til Bofaellesskab*, 137.
6. All measurements have been converted from meters and rounded off to the nearest five for readability. Therefore the meter measurements are the more precise of the two.
7. We have converted Danish Kroner (DKr) to United States dollars at an exchange ratio of 8.5:1. Exchange rates have fluctuated radically over the last decade, ranging from 4.8 DKr to the dollar to 12.6 DKr to the dollar.

In the cohousing community of Gyndbjerg, 12 houses are oriented along a small, primarily pedestrian street, which is reminiscent of villages of the past.

CHAPTER THREE

Cohousers are simply creating consciously the community that used to occur naturally.

Hans S. Andersen,
cohousing organizer

An Old Idea—
A Contemporary Approach

In many respects, cohousing is not a new concept. In the past, most people lived in villages or tightly knit urban neighborhoods. Even today, people in less industrialized regions typically live in small communities linked by multiple interdependencies. Members of such communities know each other over many years; they are familiar with each other's families and histories, talents and weaknesses. This kind of relationship demands accountability, but in return provides security and a sense of belonging. Cohousing offers a contemporary model for re-creating this sense of place and neighborhood, while responding to today's needs for a less constraining environment.

In villages, people work together to build a schoolhouse, raise a barn, harvest the crops, and celebrate the harvest. Similarly, residents in cohousing enjoy the benefits of cooperation, whether by organizing child care, common dinners, or social activities. Both communities build social relationships by working together to address practical needs.

In preindustrial communities, work is integrated with the rest of life. Small towns are not divided into residential, commercial, and industrial areas; rather, residences are built on top of shops, and cottage industries flourish throughout neighborhoods. Although cohousing developments are primarily residential, daily patterns develop that begin to weave work and home life together again. Most cohousing residents go outside the community for their professional work, but there is also informal trading of skills within the community. One resident, a doctor, tends the cuts of a child who has fallen. Another helps repair a neighbor's car. Several residents make wine together. A woman who makes pottery finds her best customers are fellow residents who buy her goods for gifts. These neighbors know each other's skills and feel comfortable asking for assistance, understanding they will be able to reciprocate later.

Technological advances make it increasingly common for people to work part time or full time at home. In most living situations today, working at home can be very isolating. The cohousing environment allows residents to enjoy the benefits of working at home without feeling isolated. As the trend toward working at home grows, cohousing communities in Denmark are considering including office space in the common facilities. Planning restrictions and financing difficulties have not permitted commercial and office space in cohousing so far, but once these issues are resolved, the model can easily be adapted to accommodate a broader range of functions.

While it incorporates many of the qualities of traditional communities, cohousing is distinctively contemporary in its approach, based on the values of choice and tolerance. Residents choose when and how often to participate in community activities and seek to live with a diverse group of people. Cohousing offers the social and practical advantages of a closely knit neighborhood within the context of twentieth-century life.

Common Characteristics

Cohousing developments vary in size, location, type of ownership, design, and priorities. Yet in our research we were able to identify four common characteristics:

Participatory Process: Residents organize and participate in the planning and design process for the housing development, and are responsible as a group for all final decisions.

Intentional Neighborhood Design: The physical design encourages a strong sense of community.

Extensive Common Facilities: An integral part of the community, common areas are designed for daily use, to supplement private living areas.

Complete Resident Management: Residents manage the development, making decisions of common concern at community meetings.

Participatory Process. One of the strengths of cohousing is the active participation of residents, from the earliest planning stages through construction. The desire to live in a cohousing community provides the driving force to get it built, and in most instances, the residents themselves initiate the project.

The number of residents who participate throughout the planning and development process varies from project to project. Often a core group of six to twelve families develops a building program, finds the site, hires the architect, and then seeks other interested people. Sometimes a large group initiates the community, and is pared down as the project becomes more defined. Typically, all of the houses are sold or rented before the project is finished. In some cases, the resident group collaborates with a nonprofit housing association or a private developer; but even then, the residents make all major decisions.

The participatory process has both advantages and disadvantages, but no cohousing has been built any other way. Even with the proven success of cohousing, developers hesitate to build it on their own. Experience shows that only people who seek new residential options for themselves will have the motivation to push through the arduous planning and design process without compromising their initial goals.

One possible obstacle is the opposition of planning commissions and neighborhood associations, usually based on false assumptions about cohousing. This is a common problem for any new development, but people's unfamiliarity with cohousing can make it even more difficult. Neighbors may fear that it will attract unconventional people, adversely affect the neighborhood, and reduce property values. Such fears are completely unfounded. Cohousing residents tend to be conscientious, taxpaying citizens, active in schools and community activities. Cohousing developments have helped to stabilize neighborhoods and make them more desirable.

Zoning laws and building codes also create barriers. Must the common house be equipped with fire sprinklers, adding sub-

stantially to the construction cost? Must the community provide the required one-and-a-half parking spaces per unit, even though residents own fewer cars? Must child care organized by the residents in the common house be classified as a commercial enterprise, conflicting with zoning regulations for residential areas?

In spite of such difficulties, resident groups have pushed their projects through the maze of barriers. When a city council denied approval of one cohousing project, the residents built models, went to meetings, and eventually convinced the council that they were respectable citizens with worthy intentions. When banks questioned the feasibility of another project, residents risked their own assets to convince the bank to give them the construction loan. When cuts had to be made to build within a construction budget, residents insisted the architect

A cohousing group discusses the final design decisions for their community.

cut the size and amenities of the individual units to preserve the common facilities. Few developers, for-profit or nonprofit, would take such risks.

Organizing and planning a cohousing community requires an enormous amount of time for group meetings, research, and decision making. Residents volunteer their time because of their commitment to the idea and their own desire for a more satisfying residential environment. The most active members are likely to attend one to four meetings a week for one, or sometimes, several years. The process can be long and frustrating, but those now living in cohousing communities universally agree that it was well worth the effort.

A feeling of community first emerges during the period when residents are working together to reach their common goal. Typically, few participants know each other before joining the group. During the planning and development phases they must agree on many issues closely tied to their personal values. Despite the inevitable frustrations and disagreements, the intensity of the planning period forms bonds between the residents that greatly contribute to the community after they move in. Having fought and sacrificed together for the place where they live builds a sense of pride no outside developer can "build into a project."

Intentional Neighborhood Design. A physical environment that encourages a strong neighborhood atmosphere is a second characteristic of cohousing. People often talk of how enjoyable it would be if they could live someplace where they knew their neighbors and felt secure; yet, few residential developments include areas where neighbors can meet casually. Cohousing residents set out to build an environment reflecting their desire for community. Beginning with the initial development program, residents

emphasize design aspects that increase the possibilities for social contact. The neighborhood atmosphere can be enhanced by placing parking at the edge of the site, allowing the majority of the development to be pedestrian-oriented and safe for children. Informal gathering places are created with benches and tables. The location of the common house determines how it will be used. If residents pass by the common house on their way home, they are more likely to drop in. In addition, play areas for small children are placed in central locations that can be watched easily from the houses or by other people in the vicinity. Parents needn't feel compelled to keep an eye on their children every minute, knowing that others will help a child in distress. By the same token, because of their central locations, play areas become meeting places for residents of all ages.

Physical design is critically important in facilitating a social atmosphere. Whether it succeeds depends largely on the architect's and the organizing group's understanding of how design factors affect community life. Without thoughtful consideration, many opportunities can be easily missed.

Common Facilities. The common house, which supplements the individual dwellings and provides a place for community activities, is the heart of a cohousing community. It is a place for common dinners, afternoon tea, children's games on rainy days, a Friday night bar, crafts workshops, laundry facilities, and numerous other organized and informal activities. The common facilities often extend beyond the common house to include barns and animal sheds, greenhouses, a car repair garage, and in one case, a tennis court and swimming pool.

These facilities provide both practical and social benefits. For instance, the common workshop replaces the need for every family

Designing a place that encourages a sense of community and allows for casual interaction among residents is an important characteristic of cohousing.

to have the space and tools to fix furniture and repair bicycles and cars. Expensive tools, such as a drill press or table saw, become more affordable when the cost is shared by several households. Not only do residents gain access to a wider range of tools through the workshop, but while working there they are likely to enjoy the company of others using the shop or just passing by.

The concept of a common space in clustered housing is not in itself unusual. Many condominium developments have a clubhouse or community room. However, a clubhouse differs from a common house both in the way the space is used and in its extensiveness. Typically a clubhouse is rented out by individual residents for private parties, or used for owner association meetings or perhaps exercise classes; it is usually limited in size, providing just enough room to accommodate occasional entertainment needs. The exception is "adult" complexes, which may incorporate a bar and a well-equipped gym into the common area. In either case, there is no place set aside for children; and most of the time the clubhouse is empty and locked. In contrast, a cohousing common house is open all day, and considered an essential part of daily community life.

As cohousing has evolved, the common house has increased in size and importance. Today, the size of private dwellings is often reduced in order to build more extensive common facilities. These changes were dictated by experience. For instance, many residents of early cohousing developments were reluctant to commit to common dinners, thinking they would be nice once or maybe twice a week, but not on a regular basis. Yet, common dinners have proven overwhelmingly successful, and today most new

In an after-school program organized by the Stavnbandet community, residents rotate supervising responsibilities.

cohousing groups plan for nightly meals in the common house, with over half of the residents participating on any given evening. Substantial space is thus allocated in the common house for pleasant dining rooms and spacious kitchens. Children's play areas are always included, and the "pillow room," reserved solely for romping and throwing pillows, has become a standard feature.

The specific features of the common house depend on the interests and needs of the residents. Their use is likely to change over time in response to new community needs. Child care may be an important function when there are many small children; when the kids are older and fewer need tending, the space may be converted to other purposes.

By allowing residents to become acquainted, discover mutual interests, and share experiences, common facilities and activities contribute greatly to the formation of a tightly knit community. These friendships then carry over to other areas. As one resident said:

The common house is an essential element. Through the activities there, life is added to the streets. Without it, the sense of community would be hard to maintain.

The common house is also an asset for the surrounding neighborhood. It is used for meetings, classes, union organizing, and day-care programs. Savvaerket residents organized a film club that attracts participants from the whole town. As the community's primary meeting place, the common house has infinite uses both for the residents and their neighbors.

Resident Management. In keeping with the spirit in which cohousing is built, residents—renters and owners alike—are responsible for its ongoing management. Major decisions are made at common meetings, usually held once a month. These meetings provide a forum for residents to discuss issues and solve problems.

Responsibilities are typically divided among work groups in which all adults must participate. Duties like cooking common dinners and cleaning the common house are usually rotated. As with any group of people, some residents feel they do more than their share while others don't do enough. This cannot be helped. In most cases, community responsibilities become less formally structured as residents become better acquainted.

Under a system of resident management, problems cannot be blamed on outsiders. Residents must assume responsibility themselves. If the buildings are not well maintained, they will have to pay for repairs. If the common activities are disorganized, everyone loses.

The process of solving problems and making decisions often involves long discussions and debates; but once an agreement is reached, it is usually respected, because everyone knows they had a say in it. People who wish to live in a community must respect the majority's opinion.

Learning how to make decisions as a group is not easy. Most people grow up and

work in hierarchical situations. Residents must learn to work together and compromise. By trial and error they learn what works. They may adopt organizational formats developed by other groups, or create new methods themselves. It is a process of learning by doing. Residents told us that over time they became more effective at working together, and applied the lessons they learned at home in their work lives. Residents sometimes choose not to participate. Some get fed up with meetings and avoid them for months at a time, then return. Others never attend meetings, but may be active in the smaller work groups. The frustrations arising from group decision making are balanced by the rewards of a community based on democratic principles.

A Unique Combination with Diverse Applications.

These four characteristics —participatory process, intentional neighborhood design, common facilities, and resident management—have come to define cohousing. None of these elements is unique, but the consistent combination of all four is. Each characteristic builds on the others and contributes to the success of the whole.

Although these characteristics are consistently present, their applications have been diverse. Each community is different because

The community kitchen at Bakken is designed for efficiency. Although meals for up to one hundred people can be prepared here, it still has a comfortable residential feeling.

Residents are responsible for all management decisions, which are discussed at common meetings usually held once a month.

each was developed by the residents to fit their particular needs and desires.

Size. While the average cohousing development accommodates 15 to 33 households, others consist of as few as two families or as many as 80. For the purposes of this book, we have focused on communities of six or more households (a division generally acknowledged in Denmark as well). We found that housing groups smaller than six households that share common areas and facilities tend to function similarly to households in which a number of unrelated people share a house or apartment.

Living in such a small community is more demanding because residents depend more on each other. If one person temporarily needs extra time to concentrate on professional interests, thereby limiting community participation, the others feel the loss. Residents must be good friends and must agree on most issues in order to live this interdependently. In addition, residents in small housing groups often have difficulty maintaining the energy to organize common activities over a period of many years. Larger

communities can more readily absorb varying degrees of participation and differences of opinion.

The average size of cohousing communities, 40 to 100 people, allows residents to retain their autonomy and choose when or when not to participate in community activities. Many people are seeking a more supportive environment, rather than a new family type. The freedom not to participate sometimes can help to create a living environment that accommodates people's changing needs over the years.

Location. Locations of cohousing developments are limited only by the availability of affordable sites. The majority are situated just outside metropolitan areas where sites are affordable and yet within reasonable distance from work, schools, and other urban attractions. Ten communities have been established in rural settings, some of them using an old farmhouse for the common house. While these developments have a "rural atmosphere," most residents still commute to nearby cities for work. Still other communities are located in the inner cities.

Design. Most cohousing communities have attached dwellings clustered around pedestrian streets or courtyards, although five consist of detached single-family houses. Eight more recent complexes have dealt with the northern climate by covering a central pedestrian street with glass, allowing access between residences and the common house without going outside.

Cohousing is generally new construction because it is difficult to create the desired relationships between spaces in existing buildings. Nevertheless, two communities, Jernstoberiet (built in 1981) and Vejgard Bymidte (1983), adapted old factory buildings, and another, Bofaelleden (1980), adapted a school building. At Jerngarden in Aarhus, residents renovated nine deteriorated row houses in 1978 to create a charming community in the inner city.

While all the newly constructed Danish developments are low-rise in scale, in both Denmark and Sweden high-rises and sections of huge housing projects have been converted to cohousing to overcome impersonal environments that encouraged vandalism and high turnover.

Types of Financing and Ownership.

Cohousing developments utilize a variety of financing mechanisms and ownership structures: privately owned condominiums, limited-equity cooperatives, rentals owned by nonprofit organizations, and a combination of private ownership and nonprofit-owned rental units. In each case, residents initiate, plan, and manage the community, whether or not the units are owner-occupied or rented. Eighteen of the 20 developments built before 1982 are completely privately financed and owned, similar to American condominiums. Since then, most projects have taken advantage of new government-sponsored, index-linked loans that structure the developments as limited-equity coopera-

tives. Five existing and six more planned projects have resulted from collaborations between nonprofit organizations and resident groups to build rental units.

Other than determining who can afford to live in the development, financing makes little difference in the actual functioning of cohousing. Thus cohousing differs from other housing categories, such as cooperatives and condominiums, which are defined by their type of ownership. Cohousing refers to an idea about how people can live together, rather than any particular financing or ownership type.

Priorities. The priorities of cohousing developments are as varied as the residents themselves. In addition to seeking a sense of community, some groups emphasize ecological concerns, such as solar and wind energy, recycling, and organic community gardens. In other developments, residents place less priority on community projects and spend more time on individual interests such as local theater groups, classes, or political organizations. Priorities often change over the years, reflecting the desires of the residents.

The cohousing communities discussed in this book evolved from the efforts of many people and reflect the different times, situations, and settings in which each development was built. Those people would be the first to say these developments should not be considered the best or only way to build cohousing, although residents do tend to be biased toward their own communities. Each project evolved from a process of weighing different options, learning from past experience, and compromising to get it built. This evolution continues today.

PART TWO

Eight Cohousing Communities:

*E*nough general discussion; let's take a closer look at some real places and the people who live in them. The following case studies give a small sampling of the variety of cohousing applications—an old factory building renovated for cohousing; a mixture of renters and owners in the same development; a glass-covered street that extends the opportunity for social interaction. Each case study emphasizes the place's special character. We begin with a close look at one community's planning process, and how they were able to design for energy efficiency.

CHAPTER FOUR

Beder, Denmark

30 Units (27 original units; three have since been subdivided into two units)

Architects: Arkitektgruppen Regnbuen

Completed: 1980

Tenure: private

Common House: 5,920 ft² (550 m²)

Sun & Wind:
Saving Energy Together

One hundred slightly anxious and genuinely curious people filled the high school meeting room one cool March evening in 1976, casually assessing each other as potential partners in the creation of a new kind of housing development. The meeting was chaired by three single mothers who sought a living environment that would serve the needs of women raising children alone. They proposed a community that would be safer for children as well as more convenient and emotionally gratifying for parents. Their quest had begun one month earlier when they placed a notice in a daily newspaper.

Cohousing Community

We are looking for people who are interested in beginning an owner-occupied housing community with a common house and common area. The residents should be of all ages, singles and families. Our hope is through common activities to create a closer community that crosses age and education boundaries.

The newspaper notice brought a deluge of phone calls. After discussing the possibilities with the interested callers, the three women set a meeting date at the high school. The majority of those attending favored a residential development that would include private dwellings and a multiuse common house. The discussion and brainstorming lasted for several hours; above all, participants expressed the desire to promote a sense of community through design.

Although single adults, married couples, and families with children represented different socioeconomic points of view, an effort was made to identify ideas that overlapped in substance and intent. A tentative proposal evolved that included shared facilities, common outdoor areas and vegetable gardens, an emphasis on community, and use of renewable energy. Some people felt that the group's direction was not collective enough; others felt it might be too collective. By the end of the evening a smaller group agreed to pursue the proposal further.

The Community Today

Sun and Wind (Sol og Vind) is best known for its use of renewable energy sources. Solar panels and a windmill fulfill 40 percent of the community's energy requirements. The houses themselves are proportionately tall to allow maximum use of solar energy and to conserve heat, but they also echo the colors and human scale of the old quarters of the nearby seaport town.

We visited Sun and Wind on several occasions five years after the residents moved in. We were particularly impressed by the community's many weekend projects. One afternoon residents were clearing the north side of the site to create a soccer field. Six or seven adults led the activities, while children joined in to unearth and wheelbarrow out the rocks. One resident commented:

Reminiscent of the colors and scale of traditional Danish villages, Sun and Wind is organized around pedestrian streets and squares. The substantial backyards of the dwellings appear even larger because there are no fences.

Although no community dinner was planned this Sunday evening (because so many people were away on vacation), residents brought their family barbecues into the courtyard for a spontaneous gathering anyway.

I sometimes envy my friends who are lounging around on the weekends sipping coffee and perusing the Sunday paper. Of course we still do that too, but there's always some project to lure me from my easy chair. Some projects are fun, others are hard work, but they all seem to foster community and help people generate their own creative energy like nothing I've ever seen before. The important thing is not to get burned out on them.

The Planning Process

From the initial newspaper ad in 1976, to the completion of construction in 1980, the proposed community underwent a lengthy process of definition and design. Because of the group's labor, Sun and Wind is a lively place today. But one cannot really describe it without first discussing the planning process—for it was in that process that the heart and soul of Sun and Wind was formed.

Defining the Goals. Through spring and summer the group kept in contact and continued discussing their ideas. By early fall,

part of the group began to coalesce with the common purpose of develop a cohousing community. Because it was clear that they would not all agree on overall intentions and on geographic location, the group split into two. In October, now reduced to seven people, one group decided to proceed by formulating their basic goals. Sun and Wind was born.

Through the winter they clarified their intentions. New people joined with the understanding that they must accept the established goals. The participants remember that spring as an optimistic and productive time; they started a newsletter, *The Wind Bag,* and formed seven work groups (site, fiscal, energy, ecology, architecture, common house, and children's interests).

In the summer of 1977, the group held a weekend retreat to discuss its progress to date, and to decide which of two geographic areas was preferred. The group was dramatically divided on the question of where to build. Half preferred the more rural area north of the city of Aarhus, while the other half preferred the suburban area south of

Future residents work with the architect on the site plan.

Sun and Wind's Development Goals

1. Approximately 25 households (with and without children) who will participate in the planning process for the community and their own individual houses.

2. Reasonable house payments to accommodate a diversity of incomes.

3. Two-story houses (to use as little land as possible) situated along pedestrian lanes and squares. Cars parked at the periphery.

4. Minimum energy consumption through planning and design.

5. Use of renewable energy.

6. Relatively small dwellings that can be easily modified and added to as needed.

7. Generous shared facilities and open space to accommodate common activities and encourage social interaction.

---

that city. The northern group, who went on to develop the cohousing community of Overdrevet, also wanted to incorporate a more progressive political orientation. Unable to agree on these issues, the group again split into two, each of 15 to 20 households. The southern group, Sun and Wind, wanted easy access to the city and to leave politics out of the discussion as much as possible. They agreed to firm up their basic aims before recruiting new members.

Preparing the Development Program.

The process of translating goals (community, renewable energy, privacy) into objectives (clustered houses, solar panels, fences) is known in architectural jargon as "the programming process." A planning committee was formed, comprising representatives from each work group, whose primary purpose was to produce a written description, or "wish list," of the community's basic intentions. With the preliminary goals identified, more specific objectives were proposed by the various work groups. The fiscal group looked into financing and legal arrangements. The common house group investigated what rooms and facilities should be included, and how large the kitchen, dining area, and playroom should be. Another group oriented new members.

The site committee met with county authorities to discuss purchasing county-owned land. The county proposed several sites, which the committee then comprehensively researched. Each site was visited, and its price and location thoroughly discussed.

In the fall of 1977, an attorney was retained to help with real-estate negotiations, agreements among residents, and other legal questions. Each member paid 5,000 Dkr ($590) to cover consulting expenses. Once a construction loan was obtained, the architects, engineers, and lawyer would be paid directly from the loan. The initiators would be reimbursed by applying their earlier contributions to the down payments on their houses.

In December 1977, members began interviewing architects experienced with cohousing and participatory design. In the end they selected a young firm, Arkitektgruppen Regnbuen, who had not designed any large projects before, let alone cohousing, but were familiar with the concept's goals. They proved extremely adept at working with the residents. The firm's enthusiasm provided what Sun and Wind needed most: architects willing to spend the time necessary for direct resident input throughout the design process.

The mechanical engineer was chosen for his experience with renewable energy sources and his willingness to include the residents in the design process. A committee was established to seek grants to help fund the extensive renewable energy systems they hoped to build.

That spring the architects and members of Sun and Wind arranged to hold a class as part of the county school district's adult education program. Meeting three hours a week for five months, they programmed and schematically designed the site plan, the houses, and the common house. The classes cost each student only 50 DKr ($5.50) and proved an effective way to subsidize a time-consuming and expensive participatory process.

The Site Plan. With a site chosen that summer, the group's first class topic was to compare their goals with the possibilities of the site. They immediately found several obvious discrepancies. The site's orientation, its vehicle access, and the group's intent to design for a sense of community all appeared to conflict with renewable energy considerations. To allow solar access to each one, the houses would have to be spread out, rather than clustered, as initially envisioned.

To clarify their objectives and to establish their priorities, the group devised a checklist of the physical possibilities for the site.

Although there had to be compromises, consistent patterns emerged. Most residents wanted centralized parking and pedestrian lanes with courtyards dispersed between the buildings. Now that clearer priorities had been established, the actual physical planning could proceed more easily.

Field trips to small towns, fishing villages, and other cohousing communities helped the future cohousers develop a common vocabulary for discussing environmental possibilities. If someone referred to the details of a courtyard that they had seen together, everyone knew what that person was talking about. "I really liked the terraces at such-and-such a place and the dining room there," someone would say.

The membership divided into four smaller groups, each with its own detailed site map and model pieces for the individual houses, common house, and parking areas. The groups initially arrived at very different designs, but with continuing discussion the models began to look more alike, mainly because of solar and community considerations. The various site plans evolved into

Initial Organizing Agreement

Purpose of the Group. The undersigned hereby form the *Sun and Wind Cohousing Organizing Group,* which is a partnership for the purpose of developing a cohousing community. The group's functions include but are not necessarily limited to exploring the scope of the proposed project as determined in future meetings; recruiting and orienting new members to the group; preparing a development program; seeking and examining potential sites.

Membership. Interested persons become active members of the group by attending three meetings, paying membership fees, and signing the organizing agreement.

To Leave the Group. Stop attending meetings and paying membership fees. [Other groups found it useful to ask for written notice from people leaving the group.]

Meetings. Minutes of discussions and decisions made will be distributed to attending and absent members before the next scheduled meeting.

Decision Making. To protect minority rights, a consensus-seeking process will be used. A formalized decision-making process [usually majority, two-thirds, or three-fourths vote] will be used only to avoid an impasse. All decisions are to be discussed thoroughly before a decision is made. Decisions can be brought up by members who were absent in the next meeting only.

Financial Obligations. The finances of the group shall be the respective obligation of all individual members. At this time the undersigned agree to pay a 20 DKr ($3) "organizing fee" each month for incidental costs which are limited to paper, mailing, photocopying, and rental of meeting rooms. For other purchases, or to incur any cost above 130 DKr ($25), authorization must be given at a regularly scheduled general meeting. No deficit may be incurred. If the group dissolves, any surplus dues will be returned to the members in proportion to the length of their participation.

The Next Step. When property is bought or other activities are undertaken that demand greater economic responsibility to the group or to a third party, the organizing group will incorporate itself accordingly.

Once incorporated, members reserve a house in the community by investing in the corporation (or partnership). Persons not able or ready to invest in the corporation may follow the project as members of the "organizing group" with the potential of buying in later if units are still available.[1]

Sketch of courtyard.

Sample from Site Plan Checklist

Traffic
- streets with cars
- streets without cars
- dispersed parking
- centralized parking

Open Area
- streets
- several small courts
- one large court

Common house location
- center of the site
- near parking
- at entrance to site

---

one, which was constructed as a large-scale model so that everyone could discuss the details. This model also proved useful in discussions about open space and the individual houses, including possible future additions, and in negotiations with local authorities about variances.

The 12 committed households (about 20 adults), the architects, and the engineer signed an agreement in December 1979, which established the newly-arrived-at site plan as the basis for future design. This agreement, endorsed by everyone, would prevent the raising of old design issues or later claims that people had not liked the design in the first place. Work could now continue in smaller groups, with all refinements based on this site plan.

The preliminary site plan was submitted to the local planning department. While they pondered this new animal, "cohousing" (with unusual features such as centralized parking and a common dining room), the future residents went about designing the individual houses.

Filling Out the Group. To secure a guarantee for a construction loan, the group needed commitments for all of the dwellings. A recruiting campaign attracted a broad variety of people. As the project began to appear more realistic, those who had been hesitant earlier took a renewed interest.

Given the massive amount of work their predecessors had accomplished, newcomers felt somewhat at a loss. To ease orientation and assimilation, each new family teamed up with an original family. One of the residents who joined at that point remembers pluses and minuses of coming in late. A personal "plus" was that he did not have to sit through the year of planning meetings, but he did miss participating in the early decisions. "I would have done things a little differently," he felt, "but that's the trade-off."

For the larger group, the now biweekly newsletter became a critical avenue of communication and cohesiveness. The work groups, the architects and other consultants were asked to report in each issue on their progress, for better or for worse.

In May 1979, encouraging news arrived from the European Economic Council (EEC) and the Danish government. Sun and Wind would receive a grant of 500,000 Dkr ($59,000) for their prototype energy system. The only stipulations were that Sun and Wind install a monitoring system to record energy savings to determine the system's applicability to other housing projects and that they be open to visitors interested in renewable energy. Unfortunately, the cost of the monitoring equipment was nearly half of the total grant. Still, this was a big lift for the group, and facilitated both recruitment of members and obtaining the construction loan. In the end, the group decided to include solar panels for space heating and domestic hot water, a windmill to generate electricity, and a solid-waste incinerator for supplemental backup heat.

The Houses. The site plan determined, the architects began to work with the residents on the design of the dwellings. Although they had initially contemplated using the same design for all houses to reduce the cost of construction, the group decided this would compromise their ability to accommodate different family sizes and incomes. Custom designing a house for each family would be too expensive. Instead they sought to create a basic core plan that could be added to, subtracted from, or otherwise adjusted to meet various household requirements.

The checklist and priority system had worked so well for designing the site plan that it was again employed to clarify members' wishes about house design. Most people preferred a small house capable of later expansion, with one and one-half levels (one level plus mezzanine) or two levels, open floor plan (combined kitchen and din-

ing room), and natural materials like wood and brick. To engage people directly in the process of designing their houses, the architects developed cardboard model kits with paper cut-out furniture, stairs, bathrooms, and even different facades.

Five basic house floor plans evolved. Residents then divided into five "house plan groups" to develop each of the models further. The paper cut-outs of dining tables, sofas, and other pieces of furniture helped them to visualize interior layouts. The architects took part in the group sessions to help residents understand the consequences of their design decisions. Throughout the process the architect used members' input to refine the site and individual house designs, always heeding cost and overall aesthetics.

By this time the design for the common house was also more clearly defined, with a large well-equipped kitchen and attached scullery, a dining room to seat all the

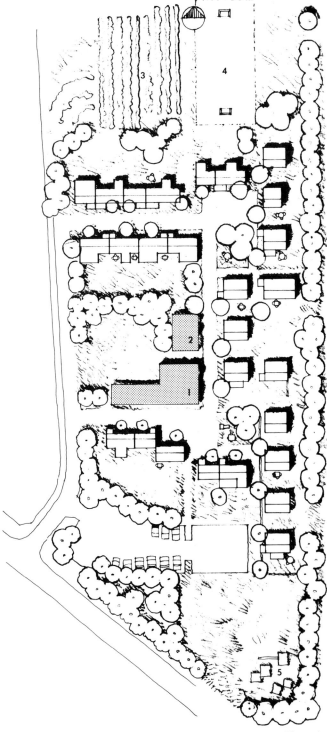

Site plan: 1. common house, 2. bicycle and tool storage, 3. vegetable garden,
4. soccer field, 5. playground.

residents, workshops, study rooms, play-rooms, laundry, auxiliary rooms, and storage rooms for the solar equipment.

The Budget. Meanwhile the fiscal group tried to keep pace with the amended decisions, inflation, and cost estimating. Among the economic policies they proposed was that the common costs of shared facilities (common house, solar equipment, land-scape, and the property) be divided in proportion to the sizes of the households; this proposal was ultimately accepted.

The evening planning class devoted its final session to the question, "Can we afford all of this?" The earlier goal of a 4,500 DKr ($530) monthly payment for a 1,075-square-foot (100 m²) house crept up to 7,500 DKr ($880) a month, owing to ambitious design revisions and rising interest rates. The fiscal group concentrated on bringing the budget back to affordable levels.

Rather than reduce construction standards to cut back costs, the residents began to favor doing part of the construction them-selves—primarily interior finishes such as cabinets, flooring, and painting. They also decided to reduce the common house area from 7,000 square feet (650 m²) to 5,920 square feet (550 m²). Finally, they decided to build 27 rather than 25 houses. Two families were already waiting to buy the lots.

The next step was to compare the incomes of the individual families with the financial consequences of what they were designing. The fiscal group wanted to esti-mate as closely as possible the impact on monthly house payments of design additions like greenhouses. Sadly, they discovered that most people would have to scale back their house designs further to make them affordable.

With the classes over, the site plan and common house design were completed by the architects and the respective work groups. The whole group confirmed major decisions. One resident remembered the participatory design process as "learning how to make critical decisions with others and gaining an immense amount of self-confidence at the same time."

To avoid conflicts it was decided that households would choose their parcels in the order in which they signed the partnership contract. The house designs were made final in meetings between the individual families and the architects, based on which core house they had chosen, which additions they planned to incorporate, and which parcel the family had purchased.

The Building Authorities. In December 1979 the project was submitted to the local building and planning departments for permits. Discrepancies with the code included gutters that drained into the yards of adjacent units (not considered a problem by the neighbors in question), and definition of the access street as a pedestrian way. Further, the code prohibited first-level windows facing directly onto the yard of an adjacent unit—a common stipulation for conventional planned-unit developments where the primary consideration is privacy. Without compromises between the building authorities and Sun and Wind, the community would have to apply for numerous variances, meaning further delays.

The authorities had never before dealt with a housing project designed and developed by the residents themselves. The planning department had always sought to protect future residents from unscrupulous speculative developers motivated only by profit. The residents of Sun and Wind were asking to do things that would normally be forbidden to developers.

The planning department could not imagine that the residents would not want to

---

Sun and Wind's Energy System

Solar: The active solar system consists of 7,000 square feet (600 m²) of liquid-filled solar panels. As many panels as possible were placed on the common house, with the rest on 15 of the houses. Two heat accumulation tanks totaling 2,600 cubic feet (73 m³) capacity are located under the common house. The 45-degree roofs are the optimum angle for solar collection at this latitude (56 degrees) and climate (cloudy winters). The heated liquid is transferred via underground pipes to the tanks under the common house. The accumulated heat is returned to the homes in the form of hot tap water and radiant space heating, again through underground pipes. The solar panels satisfy 30 percent of the community's total energy requirements.

Windmill: The 55 kw windmill satisfies 10 percent of the total energy requirements and is located one and a half miles (2 km) away atop a windy hill, mounted on a 72-foot (22 meter) tower. Danish law makes it more economical to sell the electrical energy to the power company and buy it back, rather than to consume it directly from the windmill.

Incinerator: A solid-waste (mostly wood) incinerator was designed to provide supplemental heat when the outside temperature drops to 23 degrees Fahrenheit (minus five degrees Celsius). Located in the basement of the common house, the incinerator transfers heat directly into the accumulation tank via a heat exchanger to warm domestic hot water. It was not used after the first year because it took too much work.

Central Gas Furnace: A gas furnace replaced the incinerator as backup to heat water for radiant space heating and domestic hot water.

Electricity: The local power company provides electricity for Sun and Wind's remaining energy needs.

---

drive to their own front doors. But when the authorities questioned the car-free access roads, the residents rebutted, "We can drive our cars to the door if it's essential, but it's more important to have a safe environment for the kids." Eventually their convincing arguments and a barrage of letters to planning authorities and local council members won Sun and Wind their building permit.

That same month the resident group of Sun and Wind employed a building management firm to oversee the construction—not

The private dwellings are simple, but well designed. Here we look into the kitchen from the living area of a one-bedroom, house shared by a mother and her young son.

only to help avoid costly mistakes, but also to assure that the architect was fulfilling his responsibilities. According to the architect, the project went smoothly until the management firm was introduced: "We were uncomfortable with them [the management firm] looking over our shoulders. Small problems arose that would have worked themselves out naturally, but were reported back to the group as bigger issues."

To save money, the group borrowed an old blueprint machine and reproduced the construction drawings for the bidding themselves. Over three weeks, working in shifts, 50,000 blueprints were produced—an

immensely satisfying accomplishment that saved them thousands of dollars.

Construction

Contractors were asked to submit construction bids in February 1980. The question foremost on everyone's mind was: "Will the low bid come in under our budget, or will the whole thing go up in smoke?" When the bids were all in, the lowest was still a critical $100,000 dollars above the budget that they had agreed not to exceed.

The project was feasible only if more cutbacks could be made; the alternative was to abandon the entire project and lose the

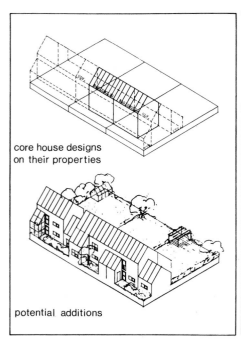

core house designs
on their properties

potential additions

TYPE B 90 m^2 TYPE B 115 m^2

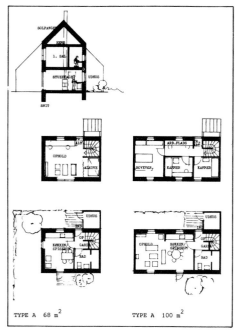

TYPE A 68 m^2 TYPE A 100 m^2

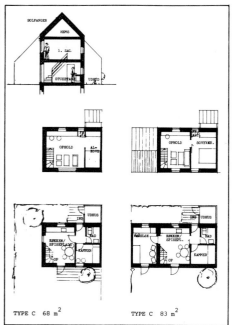

TYPE C 68 m^2 TYPE C 83 m^2

Five basic floor plans were developed from a "core house" (three are shown here), which could be expanded at the time of construction or later as the household desired. Designing for future changes allows the units to be adapted as a household's needs change, a requirement for long-term stability of the community. In recent years there have been so many additions to the houses at Sun and Wind that a resident carpenter works nearly full time on commissions from his neighbors.

Common house floor plan:
1. dining room, 2. kitchen,
3. entry and bathrooms,
4. laundry, 5. childrens'
playroom, 6. scullery, 7. pantry,
8. freezer, 9. furnace, 10. solar
and mechanical equipment,
11. workshop, 12. library,
13. game room, 14. storage,
15. crafts rooms, 16. guest
rooms and bathroom.

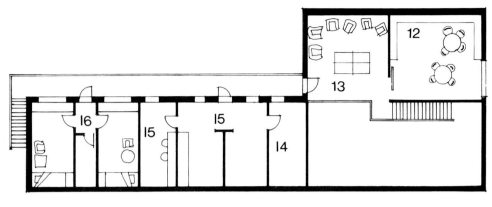

Upper Level

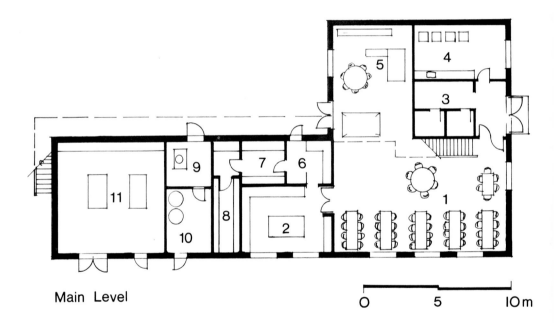

Main Level

0   5   10m

money and time already invested. Again the group turned to their consultants to find cost reductions. The architects and building management firm began intense negotiations with the lowest bidder. Construction materials, techniques, and quality were thoroughly reconsidered, and the resident-build portion was discussed. One conclusion became clear —even more standardization was required, both for the contractor and the owner-builders who would finish the houses.

They did not find any large budget items to cut, but rather small bits here and there. After a week's work they were able to wrestle the project back within budget. Now the entire group needed to decide which cutbacks were acceptable. Could they do all the landscaping themselves? Could they accept their second choice for floor materials, agree on similar kitchens [in the end they did not agree on the same kitchens and each purchased their own], and standardize the owner-build finish work? Finally, the group agreed on a revised bid of 15.5 million DKr ($1.8 million) and a 6,700 DKr ($788) monthly payment for a 1,075 square-foot (100 m²) house, and they signed the contract with the builders.

After three years of organizing, planning, and designing, construction finally began with the digging of the trenches for the foundations and underground plumbing on March 21, 1980. The residents' role now shifted from active to passive as the bricklayers and carpenters took over. The architects were responsible for daily contact with the contractor, and the resident building committee communicated concerns and criticisms in meetings with the architects and the construction management firm. Information was relayed to owners through resident meetings and the newsletter. This was a demanding period for the building committee, the architects, and the construction management firm. The tight budget could not absorb any unexpected expenses, and the construction schedule allowed little room for changes in the plans.

The first phase went relatively smoothly. By June 1980, the hopeful new residents, construction crews, architects, and all the other players celebrated the *rejsegilde* (raising of the roof—a traditional Danish celebration at the time a roof is framed, usually about halfway through construction). The contractors finished in August, two months later than scheduled. This delayed the start of the owner-build aspect of construction until the fall, when most summer vacations were over and the weather was growing increasingly cold.

Resident Construction. As planned, once the contractors finished their portion, the residents could begin to lay wood floors, finish ceilings, install kitchen cabinets and appliances, and paint.

Sun &Wind Development Timeline

Feb 76	Newspaper advertisement.
Mar 76	First meeting.
Spring–Summer 76	Discuss goals and geographic location.
Nov–Mar 77	Recruit new members. Organize committees and clarify goals. Start newsletter.
Summer 77	Planning committee formed. Site search begins.
Fall 77	Retain attorney to draw up partnership agreement and negotiate for sites.
Jan 78	Select architect.
Spring–Fall 78	Prepare development program. Site selected and schematic design for site plan completed.
Jan–Apr 79	Preliminary site plan submitted to building department. Recruit new members. Apply for construction loan.
May 79	Receive grant for solar energy system.
Jun–Nov 79	Construction drawings and cost estimates.
Dec 79	Plans submitted to building department. Construction management firm employed.
Jan–Feb 80	Construction bidding and negotiations.
March 21, 1980	Ground breaking, construction begins.
Nov 80	First household moves in.
Apr 81	All households moved in!

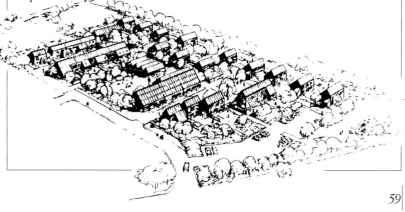

To avoid having inexperienced people working alone, three to five homeowners worked together. Each team finished one house at a time and then moved to the next house in their group. Some people became adept at installing kitchen cabinets; others became expert floor installers or painters. Although it wasn't easy, this phase fostered camaraderie and self-confidence as the residents perfected new skills.

The common house was scheduled to be completed first, so that it could augment the unfinished private houses. Unfortunately, it was only half finished when all of the houses were completed: "Because the contractors were two months behind schedule, we couldn't finish it during the week in August when we all took vacation."

The Dream Is Realized

The first family moved into Sun and Wind in November 1980. Of the more than three hundred adults who had participated in the planning at one time or another, only fifty actually moved in. The final months of construction were the most grueling. The owner-build aspect proved exhausting, con-

suming all of the residents' free time for nearly five months. Most people moved into houses that weren't quite completed, and some people had difficulty selling their previous houses.

By the spring of 1981, all had moved into their new homes, the fireside hearths were glowing with warmth, and the common house was bustling. The new residents were proud of their efforts, but they had no time to sit back and enjoy. The muddy, stark landscape had to be transformed into the parklike gardens they had envisioned. In addition, the job of feeding the solid- waste incinerator for supplemental heat was a greater task than they had imagined. It was abandoned a year later in favor of a gas-furnace hot-water heating system.

Sun and Wind is a rich and vibrant community today because their process left few stones unturned; even the smallest design questions were discussed, and they overcame whatever obstacles arose. The primary architect, Kai Mikkelsen, predicted that Sun and Wind would be the last cohousing project where the residents would spend so much time directly involved in the design.

The "street" between the houses. Residents of the 21-unit condominium development at the end of the street were so inspired by Sun and Wind that they decided to build a common house themselves.

"It's too expensive and time-consuming; future projects will seek more standardization," he commented. "As a firm, however, we learned much from the experience; now we know how to design schools *with* the teachers, and churches *with* the congregation."

This case study has focused primarily on the planning process—one of the longest for any cohousing community. Their pioneering efforts inspired others and made the work of subsequent groups easier. Not only did a neighboring cohousing community take only half the time to organize and build, but the residents of another adjacent development of 21 privately owned condominium units were so inspired that they have decided to build a common house.

Conversations at Sun and Wind

Thomas, 38 years old, married with a five-year-old son, says:

The biggest disadvantage to living at Sun and Wind is the outside attention. We get busloads of visitors, every week in the first years—Germans, Japanese, Americans, journalists—uninvited and unannounced. On some weekends there were more people wielding cameras than there were residents. What they don't understand is that cohousing is not such a radical idea; it's a little better way to live, but it does require a little extra effort to make it happen.

Tom says that the best thing about living at Sun and Wind is the sense of community. He was formerly a ship's engineer. When he returned to his hometown from tours at sea, he found that his friends and acquaintances were moving away one by one. "Finally, when I decided to settle down, I realized that I didn't have a place to return to that felt like home," he said. Sun and Wind provided a ready-made neighborhood.

Tom says that living at Sun and Wind provides "a renewed freedom. When you have children you lose some of your freedom. To move into cohousing is to regain it." He says that if he and his wife suddenly decide to go out one evening, they simply ask a neighbor to care for their son. "If they can't," he explains, "then we ask the neighbor on the other side—it's quite simple. And of course, we watch others' kids too."

Tom says that Sun and Wind was entirely too much work, especially the final stages of finishing the interiors and the landscaping: "It was becoming a negative experience; we simply couldn't see the light at the end of the tunnel. We should have planned more fun activities along the way."

Eva, a social worker, moved into Sun and Wind several years after it was built with her husband and seven-year-old son; they had previously lived in a shared house with six others. She commented:

There are disadvantages with shared living, especially the high turnover. Even though our household shared ownership, it was inherently unstable. It might be OK for an adult, but it's difficult for children—our son would just start to get close to someone when they would

Children's playroom in the common house.

By clustering the 25 dwellings in the upper portion of the site, Overdrevet has preserved the rural atmosphere the group sought when they split off from the Sun and Wind organizing group.

move. It was almost like a divorce for him. And when there was tension between a couple, the entire house felt it. Furthermore, most single-family houses aren't designed for adults to live together equally. That's why this is such a good idea. I can ignore the others if I want.

They lived in an apartment for several years but it was too isolating—especially for their son, who lacked playmates nearby:

Here we're not isolated, nor do we have to deal so much with the personal problems of others. The first year it was a bit difficult getting to know everyone, but not for Soren; kids just fit right in. Nor do I have to worry about him when he's playing outside—he has more freedom here than he would anywhere else. But, as you might expect, it takes time to get to know 50 other adults.

Overdrevet

Hinnerup, Denmark
25 Units
Built: 1980
Architect: Arkitektgruppe "E"
Tenure: private
Common House: 6,840 ft² (632 m²)

Emerging from the same initial organizing group as Sun and Wind, the community of Overdrevet was founded by participants who favored a more rural site. Located approximately eleven miles (18 km) north of Aarhus, the 25-unit community was able to retain a rural atmosphere by clustering the buildings toward the upper edge of the 6.7-acre site and leaving the rest as open space. The community maintains a large organic garden (covering one-sixth of the site), and raises chickens, sheep, and rabbits. Residents have also restored an old farm building to house crafts and woodworking workshops and a youth hangout.

Like its sibling Sun and Wind, Overdrevet utilizes renewable energy sources and energy-conserving design to minimize their energy requirements. A wind generator and solar panels provide electricity and hot water. The houses are designed to minimize exterior wall area and temperature fluctuation. Grouped in twos, threes, and fours, they employ brick thermal walls, triple-glazed windows, concrete-slab floors, and super insulation to keep heat loss 30 percent less than the maximum permitted under Denmark's stringent building regulations. These measures enable Overdrevet's households to pay less than half of what their neighbors (with comparably sized houses) pay for their energy bills.[2]

Overdrevet is the only Danish cohousing community with a strong ideological orientation, as reflected in the political cohesiveness of the group and its concern with external causes, such as national elections and Central American conflicts. While this ideological commitment nurtures a strong community sentiment in most of Overdrevet's residents, for some it becomes overbearing. A former resident commented, "You have to be strong to live in Overdrevet; there are big discussions about the 'right' way to raise children and the 'right' way to live."

In no other cohousing community we visited did residents have such strong feelings. For those who like Overdrevet, "it is the best place in the world." But it is also the only cohousing community that has had problems selling houses. Four houses were for sale when we visited in 1985; one had been on the market for two years. With so many households wanting to move out but unable to, there was considerable strain within the community. In its desire for a strong shared ideology, Overdrevet has limited its pool of potential residents. They have made this

choice consciously, and are determined to work out their difficulties without compromising their ideological stance. While Overdrevet's commitment to its founding ideals is commendable, its experience demonstrates the difference between asking residents to share facilities and to share a world perspective.

Notes
1. *Bofællesskaber Sol og Vind* (Byggeriets Udviklingsråd, 1982), Copenhagen: Statens Trykningkontor.
2. For more information on the community's energy system, see Per Madsen and Kathy Goss's article "Shared Lives, Shared Energy" *Solar Age*, (July 1982): 16–19.

With a lot of imagination and two years of sweat-equity, the residents of Jerngarden transformed an inner city junkyard and eight deteriorated row houses (left) to an urban paradise. By combining their backyards, they created a small park in the middle of the city block.

CHAPTER FIVE

Aarhus, Denmark

8 Units

Architects:
Finn Nørholm and
Ole Pedersen

Completed: 1977–78

Tenure: private

Common House:
2,010 ft² (187 m²)

Jerngarden:
Improving on City Life

I n the early 1970s, many older neighborhoods in the city of Aarhus were suffering from the woes of urban decay. Row houses and apartment blocks built in the last century desperately needed repair. Traffic clogged city streets. Families that could afford it had moved to new suburban developments on the outskirts of town, leaving behind the old, the young, and the poor. In the working-class quarter of Frederiksbjerg, residents decided something had to be done. They organized to demand commercial-traffic restrictions, new playgrounds, and loans for building renovations. Several members of the new neighborhood organization began to discuss getting a weekend cottage in the country together—"a place to escape the noise and congestion of the city."

Site plan: 1. common house, 2. storage building, 3. open space, 4. outdoor eating area, 5. typical yard of neighbors.

"But why should we be content to improve only our weekend life? It is the daily life that should be improved!" one of them recalls thinking. And they found their opportunity. New ordinances restricting truck traffic and scrap pressing within the city limits had forced the closing of an old junkyard (*jerngarden*) in the middle of the neighborhood. The junkyard's owner, who also owned eight small tenement houses surrounding the junkyard, was ready to sell.

Transforming the Junkyard

Although the group was able to purchase the site for a very good price, a vivid imagination and a lot of faith were necessary to envision what it could become. The lot was filled with the debris of 40 years as a junkyard, and the adjacent small apartments, rented to seniors, students, and retired sailors, had not been repaired in nearly as

long. Not wanting to put the present tenants out on the street, the group first directed its efforts to finding them other housing in the neighborhood. Then began two years of rebuilding.

The group, primarily young families, had no common goals other than to create a nicer place to live. They concentrated their efforts on the practical details of the building process. Two of the residents had architectural training and helped the others with their designs. Luckily, several had construction skills: among the eight households there was a mason (then studying architecture), an electrician, a plumber, and a carpenter. Each family was responsible for rebuilding its own house, but all worked closely together throughout most of the process.

The older neighbors were initially skeptical about this group of young people and their "collective" ideas. But the building process attracted their interest, and many of the locals would stop to see how construction was coming along as part of their daily routine. A resident recalls that work on the street side took twice as long as work in the back. Eventually, their impressive construction efforts earned Jerngarden the respect of even the most suspicious neighbors, some of whom still drop by.

Ten Years Later

Walking into Jerngarden today is like entering an urban paradise: charming houses with custom interiors share a park like backyard, right in the middle of the city. Of course, what one sees today results from of a lot of hard work that hasn't always gone smoothly. Focusing initially on the practical aspects of construction, the group took many years to develop its social cohesiveness. They describe their early meetings as "downright undisciplined and boisterous." Although hard feelings stemming from disagreements caused at least one family to move out, five

The community painted their houses traditional Danish colors to blend with the rest of the street.

In contrast to the hard street-scape in front of the houses, in back residents have combined their yard space to create a small park in the middle of the city block.

67

After rebuilding the exteriors of their houses, residents transformed their interiors with their own custom craftsmanship. This fireplace was built by the owner, a mason.

of the original households still remain ten years later—and those who sold their houses did so at a considerable profit.

The junkyard's office building has been converted into the community's common house, with kitchen, dining room, laundry facilities, television room (only a couple of households have their own TVs), children's playroom, photography darkroom, and workshop. Nightly common dinners were begun on a purely practical basis during the building process, and have continued ever since without any debate. A photography club, which includes people from the surrounding neighborhood, runs the darkroom. Residents are currently discussing an addition to accommodate the community's recent "baby boom."

Although all the houses have front doors facing the street, residents usually enter through the backyards, passing the common house on their way so they can see who's around. Jerngarden has little more yard space per house than its neighbors, but by combining the tiny individual yards into one big yard, they have created a much more usable space. Having a large yard where neighbors can sit in the sun and where children can play greatly enhances city living.

Jerngarden residents are still active in the neighborhood organization they helped to start. Since most of them lived in the area before, they have many friends nearby who often participate in the community's parties. A community center has been built a few blocks away, and many buildings have been renovated. Some say Jerngarden was the impetus that inspired other improvements.

We were particularly interested in residents' feelings about their community's size. "Eight households seems to be perfect," one person commented. "You know everyone well enough to keep up on what is going on in their lives." Everyone we talked with at Jerngarden shared this feeling, and

considering their location, they may be right. With the city surrounding them, residents have no lack of stimulating activities in which to take part. Whereas cohousing residents generally prefer larger communities, in the case of Jerngarden, the small number of households seems to function very well. Being so few in number may even help the community assimilate more with the neighborhood.

In the ten years of its existence, the Jerngarden community appears to have grown progressively stronger. One woman told us: "Every day when I'm riding my bicycle home from work, I think how nice it is to come home to this place. I don't know what we would do if we ever had to leave." Frankly, we wouldn't mind coming home to this pleasant community ourselves.

CHAPTER SIX

Jystrup, Denmark

21 Units

Architect: Vandkunsten

Built: 1984

Tenure: Cooperative

*Common House:
4,350 ft² (404 m²) plus
8,560 ft² (795 m²) of
covered street*

Jystrup Savvaerket:
Glass, Color, and Community

Like the country itself, cohousing in Denmark has two personalities —summer life and winter life. Residents often complain that socializing decreases significantly during the long, cold winters. People cannot sit around outdoors, and the inconvenience of having to don boots and coat to go outside greatly reduces use of the common house. Architects of cohousing have responded by designing glass-covered pedestrian streets.

But the street! Nobody can imagine how we could function without it—here there is life all year round. Here we sit, talk, and drink coffee 'til one in the morning, here the kids play when it rains or snows. The glass-covered street is simply one of the best parts of our house.

The common house sits at the junction of the two covered streets with a library in the highest tower. Private decks, which extend over the roof of the covered street, and ground-level patios provide every household with a sunny, private space facing the shared outdoor area.

As one of its residents enthusiastically comments, the narrow, blue-walled, glass-covered street at Jystrup Savvaerket ("the Jystrup Sawmill") is a great success. Completed in 1984, this community has 21 residences arranged along two covered pedestrian streets that meet at the common house. (This site plan is similar to Trudeslund, but with the buildings connected by a giant skylight.) Not only the common house, but the whole street becomes an extension of the private living spaces, serving as a vestibule for coats and boots, a play area, and a gathering place—essentially the

community's living room. "I can walk up to the common house in my slippers any time of year," a resident remarks. Including the covered street and the common house, more than 40 percent of Savvaerket's developed area is allocated to common use.

Located at the junction of the two perpendicular residential wings, the common house is separated from the unheated covered street by a glass wall, so that one can see directly in from either wing. On the ground floor, a fireplace and sitting area overlook a south-facing terrace. Half a level down are a professionally equipped kitchen and a comfortable dining area. Four rooms upstairs accommodate a variety of uses; currently, two are used for the child-care program, one is a youth hangout, and the other has a billiard table. In the tower is a library. "In the future, maybe we'll rent out rooms for a teenager to live in or for someone who wants to work at home," one resident speculates. The mailboxes, located near the entrance from the upper parking lot, bring many residents through the common house on their way home from work.

Other common facilities—a workshop, a laundry room, and two "supplementary" rooms—are located along each of the two covered streets. One workshop is used for wood and metalworking, the other for textiles. Despite the residents' initial skepticism, one washing machine for each wing has proven quite sufficient. A previously existing

The covered street creates a rich, new living pattern resulting from the overlapping of private and community space. Residents have placed their extra furniture from larger previous houses in the street for all to enjoy.

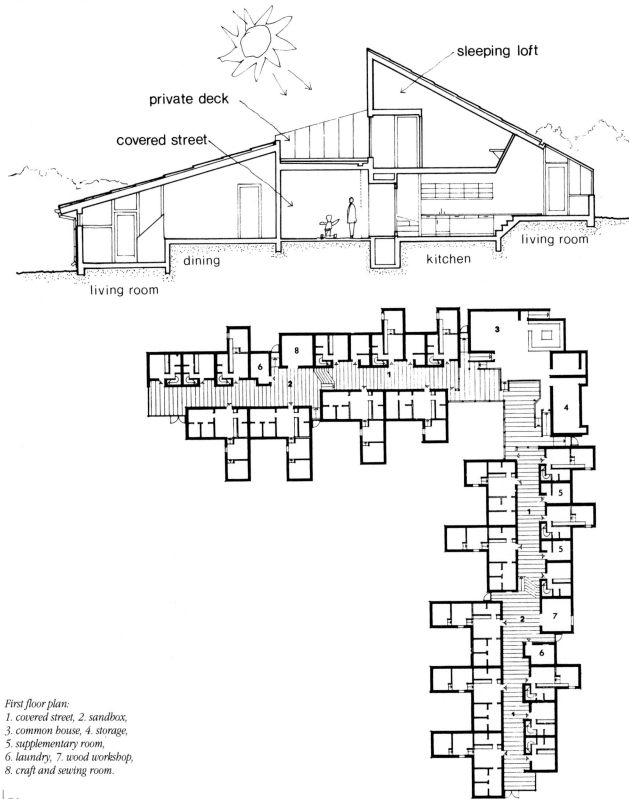

sleeping loft

private deck

covered street

living room

dining

kitchen

living room

First floor plan:
1. covered street, 2. sandbox,
3. common house, 4. storage,
5. supplementary room,
6. laundry, 7. wood workshop,
8. craft and sewing room.

West Elevation. The architects combined traditional Scandinavian forms and building materials (wood was traditionally stained with a black preservative paint) with unique uses of contemporary materials (prefabricated corrugated roofing is also used as sheathing on the exterior and covered-street walls).

Community child care allows Savvaerket's youngest to stay home all day long; their older brothers and sisters will join them after school.

building is used for an auto repair shop and storage.

The supplementary rooms, or "S-rooms," are one of Savvaerket's innovative features. Each just over two hundred square feet, with its own bathroom, the S-rooms are used as guest rooms, office space, or teenagers' bedrooms. For instance, one family found that living with three children in their small dwelling was too cramped. By renting the S-room next door for a few years, they gave their teenage daughter more privacy, and everyone retained their sanity. A mother of two used another S-room to study for her architectural exams. The covered street makes access between the S-rooms, the dwellings, and the common house as easy as walking down the hall, and the flexibility of these rooms allows maximum use of the extra space every household occasionally needs.

Sixteen of the community's children participate in the child care and after-school program. The parents hire three teachers (none of whom live there) to run the program, but supervise it closely themselves. Not only is full-time community child care convenient, but it makes use of the common

facilities during the otherwise quiet daytime hours when most adults are away at work.

Nightly common dinners were one of the priorities of Savvaerket's initiators. Steffen, an enthusiastic resident, comments:

Our dinner system has functioned perfectly from the beginning. We get a good and varied diet. Everyone's ideas and gastronomic abilities can be tried—with varying success, of course. But it functions well and we eat cheaply.

Five or six adults are responsible for planning and preparing dinners for a week at a time. With seven rotating groups, each resident helps prepare dinner for only one week out of seven. Within the group people trade responsibilities to fit their interests and schedules; someone who gets home early might do the cooking, and another who gets home late cleans up. All households participate, choosing between plan A for all 30 dinners a month or plan B for 20. Dinners average a dollar for an adult and half price for children under twelve, paid at the beginning of the month.

Our own experience at Savvaerket further confirmed the success of common dinners. Because of the summer holidays, the evening we arrived in August was one of the few nights no common dinner was planned; yet everyone spontaneously decided to bring their dinners out to eat together in the covered street. After dinner, we enjoyed our glasses of wine and conversation late into the summer night.

The Private Dwellings

Early in the planning process the initiators decided to maximize the common areas and minimize private residences. As a result, the one-, two-, and three-bedroom dwellings range in size from 680 to 1,045 square feet (63 to 97 m²); their average size is 10 per-

Each household has its own private yard.

cent less than the maximum allowed under cooperative financing laws, with the extra space going to the common areas.[1]

Two-story units line the outer sides of the street, with one-story units on the inner sides. Private decks extending over the street and ground-level patios provide every house with a sunny, private outdoor area. From the covered street, one enters directly into the kitchen-dining area, leaving coats and boots in the common area outside the door. Since residents eat most of their dinners in the common house, the private kitchens have only two-burner stoves.

The architects did an exceptional job of utilizing every square foot of space, as well as designing spatially interesting living areas. High ceilings allow for extensive use of sleeping and storage lofts, which add as much as 15 to 20 percent to the usable floor area of the house. Though small, these high-quality dwellings offer a variety of enjoyable spaces, both indoors and out.

The Development Process

After hearing about the planning processes of other cohousing groups, Savvaerket's initiators decided to limit their group to eight households until most of the initial planning was completed. They found an ideal site in the small town of Jystrup, 30 miles (50 km) from central Copenhagen. Although county officials encouraged the group, the town's seven hundred residents were suspicious of the project and its unconventional development ideas. However, a declining school population was threatening to close the local school, and when the townspeople realized that 21 new households would bring enough children to keep the school open, their protest quieted. But then the local government decided not to sell the building site originally chosen, and it took another year to redesign for a second site.

Architect Jens Arnfred, of Vandkunsten Architects, led the group through a dynamic design process. Vandkunsten has always

Small kitchens equipped with two-burner stoves are sufficient because residents eat most dinners in the common house.

been a strong advocate of resident participation, but they do not play a passive role. Arnfred remembers:

I told them [the Savvaerket group] *that they had to take the consequences of what they were doing, that they were pioneers, and that if they really believed in their ideals they had to live up to them architecturally.*

From the other side, a resident recalls:

Jens [Arnfred] *pushed us very hard. Many of us had doubts and resented him pushing. . . but he earned our respect and we learned to trust him. He could not have taken such a strong approach if we didn't trust his judgment.*

It was not until late in the design that anyone knew in which house they were going to live. This eased the process, since decisions were based on the common good, rather than on individual desires.

The unconventional design of Savvaerket made it even more difficult to get the necessary approvals. The covered street had to be explained and justified to the Ministry of Housing, the building department, and financing institutions. The group's architects and lawyers were familiar with the cohousing development process, having worked together on Trudeslund and separately on other cohousing projects; this helped to push the design through the bureaucratic hurdles. Still, it took nearly four and a half years of meetings to get the project built.

Jystrup Savvaerket Today
Was it worth it? Absolutely, the residents agree; the advantages far outweigh any problems. During our visit we persistently looked for evidence that the residents might be uncomfortable with the interior street and

the resulting proximity of private and common areas. But no one seemed to doubt the success of the design. "We respect each others' needs for privacy and time alone. There are unspoken signs to show that you want to be alone, like closing the curtains, and those signs are respected by the others," a resident explained. Of course the impulse to socialize can itself create a problem: "It is difficult when I have to get some work done. If I know people are out in the street talking and drinking coffee, naturally I'd like to join them," commented one resident.

Conversations at Savvaerket

Annie and Steffen Lenschau-Teglers first discussed living in a community with friends 20 years ago: "How could we help each other more? We turned the thought over many times with friends, but it never became realizable. We bought a little house and then a larger one, had two children, and finally resigned ourselves to only dreaming of living in a cohousing community."

Then one day a friend called to say his family had joined the Jystrup Savvaerket group in planning a new cohousing community. Would they like to join? It was a dream come true. As one of the core families, they participated in more than three years of weekly meetings and spent many long nights working out the details of the project.

Asked if they have any regrets about moving from a large single-family house to a 1,045-square-foot residence, Annie says, "No, we're really glad we did it. Jystrup is a little far from central Copenhagen for our preference, but we wanted to try a new way of living, and this community is a wonderful place to live."

Notes
1. The cooperative financing law requires that the average dwelling size not exceed 1,023 ft² (95m²) to qualify for financing.

Annie, a librarian, and Steffen, a journalist currently working for a public-relations firm, with their two children, Mikkel (14) and Signe (11), were one of the first eight families to join the Savvaerket group.

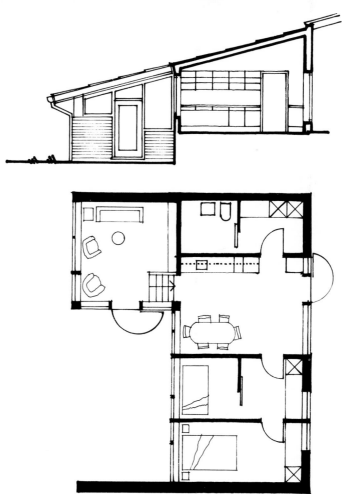

Two-bedroom unit floor plan; 750 ft² (70 m²).

CHAPTER SEVEN

Mejdal I

12 Units

Holstebro, Denmark

Architect: Niels Christian Andersen

Completed: 1979

Tenure: private

Common House: 2,150 ft² (200 m²)

Mejdal I & II:
One Leads to Another

Architect Niels Christian Andersen had not yet heard of cohousing when he and his family first talked with two other families about building a cluster of houses with shared facilities. All three families had small children, and buying a house in the suburbs seemed the logical next step in their lives, although they had some reservations about the suburban lifestyle. Initially they doubted whether they could find others in the provincial northwestern corner of Denmark who would share their interest in such a housing development. They decided to give it a try, however, and in two years not only had they succeeded, but their success led to the development of a second community next door.

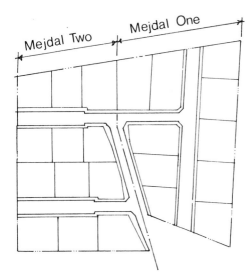

Both Mejdal sites were initially planned as typical subdivisions for speculative "tract" homes. The cohousing groups' proposals included more houses, but they were able to save the trees and provide more open space by reducing paved area.

Mejdal I site plan:
1. common house, 2. carport,
3. bicycle shed, 4. play area,
5. vegetable garden,
6. greenhouse addition.

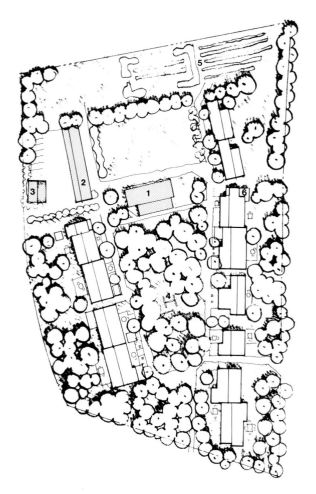

From the outset the Mejdal group concentrated on practical issues. The first step for the three families was to write a letter to three realtors outlining their requirements for a site:

- large enough for approximately 12 houses with natural amenities such as trees
- adjacent to existing development
- within cycling distance of town
- available within a year
- could be within an already subdivided area, but without roads and storm drains installed
- no planning code requirement to use electric heating
- as inexpensive as possible

They found a beautiful tree-covered site at the edge of a recently developed subdivision of single-family houses. The site had already been surveyed into ten standard parcels. Upon locating the land in May 1977, the group called a public meeting, which attracted 25 families. Despite this initial interest, only five households were ready to invest when it was time to actually buy the site seven months later. A long debate ensued about whether they should proceed, which was settled when Niels Christian Andersen suggested that his architecture firm could develop the remaining sites, thereby relieving the group of the risk.

To lower the cost per unit, the group proposed locating twelve rather than ten houses on the property, while still saving most of the trees. The removal of trees in the original subdivision proposal had been a point of contention between the county and the surrounding neighborhood, who wanted to save the wooded grove, and Mejdal's proposal proved propitious. With Andersen as the architectural consultant, the group developed simple guidelines for the 12 houses. To

A walkway circles the central wooded area around which the houses are situated.

encourage harmony in the design, they agreed that all the houses should use red brick on the exterior and have red tile roofs. No house was to exceed 2,150 square feet (200 m²); upon completion, the houses ranged in size from 1,185 to 1,775 square feet (110–165 m²).

Each house was designed individually by Andersen, who worked with each family to meet its needs, tastes, and budget. All the houses share certain common traits. Each is designed with a heavy masonry "central spine" to store heat and to moderate temperature fluctuations. Oriented around a wooded open space, the houses were designed to be "friendly toward the front," with windows facing the common area, and a small semi-private sitting area. Great care was taken to make the rear terraces private, nestled

among the trees. By the time construction began, all the parcels were sold. Since the original construction was completed, greenhouses have been added to many of the houses.

The contractor built the small brick portion of the common house, containing the laundry and furnace facilities, before commencing on the houses. Using logs from the site, the residents built the rest of the common house themselves, finishing it just after the houses were completed. "There were some of us who thought that we couldn't do it, that we'd better have it hired out . . . but we built it," exclaimed one proud resident. The "homemade" solar panels on the common-house roof are used to preheat hot water for the individual houses and provide floor heat.

Mejdal I's 2,150-square-foot (200 m²) common house includes 1,720 square feet (160 m²) of solar panels on the roof, with a kitchen, dining room, sitting area, children's play area, workshop, and sauna inside.

Residents prepare for a special dinner in the common house, which they built themselves using trees from the site.

The residents of Mejdal I estimate that their houses cost approximately 20 percent less than comparable single-family houses. A major factor in the lower cost was that fewer site improvements were required. It was not necessary to build roads and driveways, since the residents walk to their homes from the gravel parking lot. Because there is no pavement, an extensive storm drainage system is not necessary; they rely more on natural water seepage and runoff. Acting as their own contractors, the residents were able to pool resources to find the least expensive materials, and to buy in bulk. Mejdal also included two more houses than the site was originally zoned for, so there were more people sharing the cost of the land. There was no developer's profit margin (which can be 20 percent by itself), and no marketing expense (usually 6 percent), because the houses were presold before

Mejdal I's workshop is well laid out, efficient, and easy to clean. Residents use the workshop frequently, yet it is always kept neat. This orderliness is maintained by a unique system of accountability. Users pick up the keys from specific individuals in charge of the shop. If someone does not clean up, it is an affront to these individuals personally, rather than to the more anonymous larger group.

they were built. No tacked-on features, such as lattice-work fences, were required to make the homes "salable"; the residents determined just how much "curb-appeal" they needed. No interest charges accumulated on the loan while the finished houses sat empty awaiting sale. Moreover, the residents are realizing ongoing savings due to the passive solar design and active solar heating system, as well as the many other economies inherent in cohousing.

Conversations at Mejdal

Niels Christian Andersen, architect and Mejdal's initiator, married with three children, commented:

It's not the practical advantages of living in cohousing that are most important to me. It's the sense of belonging, a real home; I need the community as a safe harbor to come home to after a trying day. What I like about cohousing is that I can choose to use it when I want it—it's there when you need it, but not forced on you.

Making Workshops Successful

It may be hard to imagine that a workshop used by 50 or 60 persons could possibly function smoothly. Potentially, a shared workshop can help residents save money and produce better work, and it can be more fun in the process. It can also be a chaotic free-for-all. In comparing the systems of different cohousing communities, we found that the following practices promoted the usability and safety, and decreased the frustration, of a shared workshop:

A. Accountability. Keeping the workshop locked and having two or three people "in charge" makes users feel accountable to the person they get the key from, who will be upset if a tool is missing or the shop is left messy.

B. Buying in, or varying degrees of investment. Some may want to have better power tools; they should buy and store them separately in a locker or tool box. Others may not even want to invest in a good set of hand tools (and should not plan on borrowing them). Thus, there can be two or three levels of investment. (Cohousers generally advise against various levels of investment for common facilities except when a small group wants to purchase something that less than half of the residents are likely to use, such as a table saw or a sailboat.)

C. Children. Some feel that children should have full access to the workshop (except power tools), to encourage their spontaneous creativity. For safety and to prevent abandoned projects, others feel that children should be permitted only under adult supervision. Between the permissive and disciplinarian attitudes there is a practical middle ground. Adults should aggressively teach interested children "shop manners"—safety first, how to clean up, and how not to abuse tools. Once they have demonstrated competent shop manners, children should be given equal access. Until then, they might have a separate bench, with their own tools.

D. Day-Glo. Successful workshops paint their hand tools the most awful Day-Glo fluorescent colors available, "so you can see those suckers 50 yards away lying in two feet of grass." Besides, no self-respecting person would want tools that color in their house.

The architect worked with each household on the design of its house. The simple and clean tradition of Scandinavian design shows throughout.

As the architect and a resident, it's important to establish the boundaries between work and private life. Since I was the first to move in, I was right here during all the construction. I had to ask people to call me during office hours at work if they wanted to discuss their house. Luckily there were few enough houses that I was able to finish before my practice went broke.

The planning process was exhilarating. We set a time limit of one year to plan the development. I knew if we didn't work fast, we would lose people. When you're in the middle, you say absolutely never again. But when you're finished you only remember the good; it really was great fun. Decisions were so much easier then; we had to move quickly. Now it takes forever to make the smallest decisions. Some day I would like to live closer to a larger city, with other cohousing communities nearby . . . like pearls on a string.

Frede Dyblijaer, teacher of computer science, married with three children, observed:

If I had to choose one word to describe what cohousing means to me, it would be "security"—in the emotional sense that I know there are people that I can depend on, people I can call for help. When I couldn't make it home the other night, I called a neighbor to ask him to feed the chickens. When I got home I found that he had not only fed the chickens but also the rabbits, figuring that I had forgotten about them.

We never worry about finding a baby sitter because we know we can depend on one of the neighbors—and the kids are very comfortable staying with them. The older kids can just stay home because they have neighbors to call if they have any problems.

Mejdal II

14 Units
Holstebro, Denmark
Architects: Niels Christian Andersen and
Per Pedersen
Completed: 1985
Tenure: private
Common House: 1,600 ft² (150 m²)

A second community, Mejdal II, was started by four families who grew impatient waiting to buy a house at Mejdal I after it became apparent that resale opportunities would be scarce, at best. When Niels Christian Andersen heard that the site adjacent to Mejdal I was available, he organized the people on the waiting list. The Mejdal II site had also already been subdivided into single-house parcels. Yet, again, local plan-ning authorities allowed an increase in the number of houses, this time from 12 to 14. When the economy turned downward and interest rates climbed sharply, the four families had problems finding ten other buyers. The cohousing sites were finally sold one at a time, with almost five years between the completion of the first and the last houses.[1]

The organization of the community was delayed by the extended construction schedule and by the fact that many of the residents built their own houses. Construction of the common house did not begin until the individual houses were completed. Although three dinner clubs met in private houses, one resident says, "It wasn't until we planned and started building the common house and landscape improvements that we came together as a community."

Mejdal II was built on the site next to Mejdal I.

Suburban Cohousing

Some would criticize Mejdal I and II for being just middle-class suburban houses. Yet it is just that conventionality, with only a slight departure from the mainstream, that makes these developments so interesting. Here a group of ordinary families has created a place that suits their needs better than anything else available on the market. Like other cohousing communities, Mejdal I presented a positive example for others to follow. Together they were able both to create a sense of community where one may not have otherwise developed and to save a grove of trees that would have been lost. Together they are able to incorporate a renewable energy system, which would have been too expensive and inconvenient to do individually. Most importantly, living in a supportive environment enhances people's quality of life and allows them to contribute more positively to the larger society.

Notes
1. Mejdal II is the only cohousing development that did not initially build the total number of dwellings planned. Other communities had commitments for each dwelling by the time construction was completed, even if only half were spoken for when construction commenced.

Mejdal II site plan: 1. common house, 2. carport, 3. play area.

A child works with one of his neighbors as residents prepare to pour the concrete for the floor for their common house.

Residents converted this old iron foundry to a 21-household cohousing community. The private dwellings are located in the shed-roofed wings with the central hall serving as an interior courtyard. The common house is situated at one end of the central hall with exterior decks facing the shared outdoor area.

CHAPTER EIGHT

Roskilde, Denmark

21 Units

Architects:
Jan Gudmand-Høyer
Jes Edvards,
Helge Christiansen

Completed: 1981

Tenure: private

Common House:
3230 ft² (300 m²) plus
a 6500 ft² (600 m²)
interior court.

Jernstoberiet:
From Iron Foundry to Cohousing

What do you do with a 1946 iron foundry when the company closes down? The planning department in the town of Roskilde assumed the concrete structure would have to be bulldozed, and proposed rezoning the site for 14 detached single-family houses. But that was before the building was discovered by a group looking for a site on which to build a cohousing community. Today the original structure still stands, renovated to accommodate 21 residences and a common house, with the large central hall of the foundry providing an interior courtyard for play, festivals, and informal gatherings.

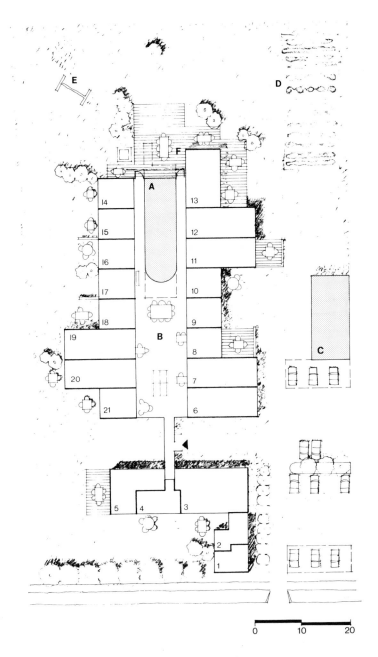

Site plan: A. common house,
B. interior court, C. storage and
workshop, D. vegetable garden,
E. Play ground, F. terrace.

Planning and Design

Jernstoberiet ("the foundry") was one of
several communities initiated through the
efforts of SAMBO, an organization established to bring people interested in cohousing together and provide groups with technical assistance. Upon hearing about the

foundry site, several members of SAMBO
immediately began to organize a group
interested in developing cohousing there.
One of these initiators was Flemming
Hagensen, a research technician, who with
his wife, Ingrid, a school secretary, was
ready to give up the single-family house
they had owned for 20 years as soon as his
daughters left home. In an interview for
SAMBO'S newsletter, Hagensen discussed
the shortcomings of the single-family house:

*Contact between neighbors dwindles as
soon as the hedges grow up between the
houses. . . . In any case, I have no doubts,
after watching my parents become more
and more isolated behind their hedges as
they get older, and I think it won't be
many years before I could be sitting just
like them.*

Not wanting to spend the rest of his life
isolated behind his hedges, Hagensen
focused his energy on organizing the
cohousing community—talking with officials,
recruiting potential residents, and attending
meeting after meeting. Financial realities dictated a tight timeline, and finding people
willing to invest in the project at this early
stage was a constant concern. "Most people
want to wait until there is a finished project,"
Hagensen remarked. He explained that one
of the main objectives for the design of
Jernstoberiet was to encourage:

*different forms of unorganized activities
. . . with a place you can just drop in
when you want to be with other people.
Not so that on Thursday at such-and-such
a time . . . but so there is life in the common house—a newspaper reading room,
a cafe, a hobby workshop, or table tennis.
Primarily, a place to go when you have
the desire and energy to move from your
own armchair.*

The front doors of the dwellings open onto the interior court.

The first design proposal called for demolishing the large foundry building and reusing only the one-story office building at the front of the site. Architect Jan Gudmand-Høyer then developed a second scheme with his students at the Architecture Academy in Copenhagen. They proposed reusing the main building; not only would this eliminate the costs of demolishing the huge concrete structure, but it would also create a unique opportunity for an exciting living environment. The local planning department supported the proposal enthusiastically.

In utilizing the large central hall as an interior courtyard, Jernstoberiet was the first cohousing development to combine individual residences and common facilities under one roof. (Glass-covered street schemes, increasingly popular in recent years, had not yet been built.) Individual residences, located in the shed-roofed wings of the structure, line the central hall like row houses. Each residence has its own garden on the outside, with a main entrance off the central hall on the inside. Five additional residences are located in a newly built annex, which is connected to the central hall by a covered walkway.

Reusing the old structure entailed many unusual considerations, particularly how to bring it up to current residential building codes. Moreover, the building department had no precedent for an interior courtyard. Initially, the design included operable windows and glass doors between individual residences and the central hall to reduce the barriers between private and common areas.

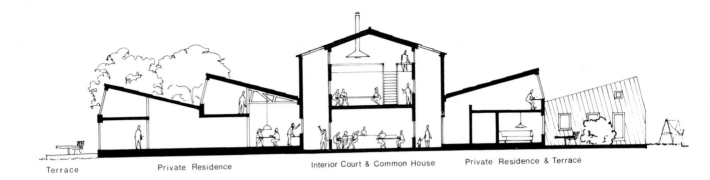

Terrace   Private Residence   Interior Court & Common House   Private Residence & Terrace

Section through building.

Enjoying the afternoon sun.

The common facilities were also originally designed as terraces open to the hall. But the building department required compromises to meet fire codes, allowing only a limited number of fixed windows between private and common interiors, and requiring that the shared facilities be enclosed in a separate house within the hall.

To reduce costs, residents did much of the demolition and construction themselves. Weekends and vacations were spent tearing out interior walls, sorting out reusable materials, and hauling the rest to the dumpster. Residents also did much of the interior finish work, including painting, laying the flooring, and installing kitchen cabinets. After moving in they completed the landscaping and built carports and storage sheds.

Community Life Today
Since moving in during the summer of 1981, Jernstoberiet residents have found numerous uses for the central hall—as a vestibule, a play area for kids on rainy days, a badminton court, a festival hall, and an extended living room for the whole community. Though unheated and quite cool during the coldest winter months, the interior court always provides a dry place for residents to chat as they come and go during the day.

The dining room is located in the common house at the end of the hall. Here dinner is served four to six times a week, with 50 to 60 percent of the residents (25 to 35 people) typically taking part. The use of tokens, earned by cooking, assures that people prepare dinner in proportion to the

Residents enter through the central hall, which provides a covered courtyard for playing and socializing.

95

The evening's chefs prepare dinner in the common house.

number of times they eat. Each month residents sign up for when they will cook, and a few days beforehand, for when they will be there for dinner. This flexible system allows residents to participate as much or as little as they like.

Upstairs from the dining room are a children's playroom, a television room, and a large sitting and crafts room. The latter serves as a sort of community "family room," with daily newspapers, a library, and a fireplace, as well as tables for sewing and crafts. Many of the women leave their sewing machines and materials here, where plenty of work space and often good company are available.

We noted that not having to go outside to get from one's house to the common house greatly encourages the spontaneous use of this workroom. In other communities we have observed that the psychological barrier of having to put on boots and coat on a dark, cold night often keeps people at home unless a specific activity is planned.

The Residents and Their Dwellings

A wide range of individual dwelling sizes, from 410 to 1,370 square feet (38 to 127 m²), accommodates a variety of incomes and household types. With more than half the units 690 square feet (64 m²) or smaller, Jernstoberiet was one of the first privately financed cohousing developments to successfully recruit a substantial number of single adults. Of the 21 households, six are single adults, one is a single parent, three are couples without children, and the other eleven are families with children at home. At our last count, this included 35 adults and 18 children, ranging in age from zero to 56.

While the existing concrete structure defined the size and form of the individual units, residents had considerable flexibility in laying out their interiors, so that today no two are the same. Only the location of stairs and bathrooms is standardized. Although it would have saved money to have the same kitchen layout throughout, the residents could not agree on one design, and they ended up allocating a budget for each household to finish its own kitchen. All the kitchens except one face the central court. The shed-roofed form brings light deep into the interiors and allows for large lofts, greatly increasing the living space. Building additions are possible in all of the units.

By reusing the existing structure, keeping individual units small, and doing much of the work themselves, Jernstoberiet residents were able to develop one of the most affordable privately financed cohousing communities built at the time (new financing possibilities since 1981 have assisted later developments). Although development costs were considerably higher than initially estimated, the selling prices were still within the budget of moderate-income households—no small feat in a period of very high interest rates.

This unusual project did present unique complexities in determining the price of each unit and its share of the common facilities. After some debate residents finally agreed on a calculation which considered not only unit size but also orientation and household composition, with dwellings on the south side costing more.

One sign of Jernstoberiet's success is that a new community, Ibsgarden, was started by people from the waiting list who gave up waiting. Unable to buy the factory building they originally wanted near Jernstoberiet, the group purchased another site nearby.

Summing up the virtues of Jernstoberiet, resident Flemming Hagensen observed after his first few years of living there:

> *I think it functions fantastically well—not without problems, but with problems that I would much rather deal with than those one has in an ordinary isolated house.*

During the planning stages of Jernstoberiet, Flemming Hagensen explains a model of the project at a housing exhibit where the group recruited several new members.

The common house is located at the end of the central hall.

CHAPTER NINE

Birkerød, Denmark

Six Units

*Architects:
Arkitektgruppen*

Completed: 1978

Tenure: private

*Common House:
2,045 ft² (190 m²)*

Tornevangsgarden:
Small Can Be Beautiful Too

Tornevangsgarden, "the Thorny Field Farm," is the smallest cohousing community we will discuss in this book. We include it not only to point out some of the characteristics of small-scale cohousing, but also because it was one of the inspirations for this book. Here is how Charles remembers it:

While attending school in Copenhagen, I walked past a group of six houses on my way to the commuter train station. Each day, I wondered what made them different, and why I enjoyed them so. The houses were set in three pairs around a courtyard. People came and went from a seventh, larger building; they might be carrying laundry, wheeling a bicycle, or simply empty-handed. I could see youngsters running about, and people sharing a pot of tea or just sitting and conversing at the picnic table. Some nights the lights were on inside the larger building, and it appeared that all of the residents were eating dinner together.

Finally, curiosity prevailed and I walked up to one of the houses. Through the window I could see a middle-aged woman working in the kitchen. I knocked on the front door, and in my best but still terrible Danish I asked if she would tell me something about this place. Amused by my attempt to speak Danish, she graciously took an hour to tour the grounds and the common facilities with me. In her own house she explained, in perfect English, that the "busy" side of the residence is toward the courtyard in front, and the private side is toward the rear.

Like many other cohousing developers, the residents were motivated to develop Tornevangsgarden by the bustle and impersonality of contemporary living. The woman told me:

It got to the point that we had to make appointments to see our friends: "Let's get together some time next month." Even that became increasingly infrequent; we were drifting away from the very people that we appreciated and enjoyed being with most. Friendship, a more spontaneous environment, and the notion of shared child rearing motivated us most.

Aerial of Tornevangsgarden with the six houses oriented around a courtyard and the common house (the old farmhouse) near the front of the site.

Tornevangsgarden (or "Torn," if it's easier) was my introduction to cohousing, and Kathryn and I returned four years later to get the whole story.

An Ambitious Beginning

Originally, the four organizing families had attempted to find a site large enough for 20 to 30 houses. Each site they looked at had a flaw—it was too far from town, or it needed to be rezoned, or had some other problem. Economic considerations ruled out too long a search for a site. "The risk was already high," said one resident. "Normally a builder attracts buyers who can afford what is already built. We, on the other hand, had to build what we could afford, based on fixed incomes and prices that were rising monthly during those high inflationary times [about 12 percent annually]." The four families finally bought the present site in 1976, after a one-and-one-half year search. "We didn't choose to have only six houses," said one resident. "We simply became impatient with looking for a larger site and settled (quite literally) on what we could find."

Only five blocks from the center of the small town of Birkerød (pop. 20,000), Tornevangsgarden was once the site of a farm. The lush grounds had a bucolic nineteenth-century charm, including a half-timbered, thatched-roof farmhouse (now the common house), old fruit and shade trees, and a tranquil pond. It is just a 10-minute walk to the bus and commuter train station and a 15-minute walk to the public school.

The Design

The initiating group selected Arkitektgruppen, a young firm with previous experience designing cohousing communities, to do the design. Child care was a major consideration in the site layout. The houses are oriented around a small court, which allows parents to keep an eye on small children playing

there. Today, most of Torn's small children have become teenagers, so a picnic table and flower boxes have replaced the sandbox, and real teacups have replaced the toy ones once filled with sand.

Four of the six houses have their kitchen/dining rooms facing the court. The more private living areas and bedrooms look out on private rear yards and gardens, beyond which lie the pond and the larger common garden areas. The other households quickly pointed out to us that they now wish they had situated their kitchen/dining rooms toward the courtyard, as the others had.

Each house is situated on its own 1,500-square-foot (140 m²) lot. The rest of the area is owned in common; by agreement, families may build additions on one another's lots or onto the common area. The houses cost an average of about 568,650 DKr each ($66,900). Each house's price was determined by its square footage and number of bathrooms. The final cost exceeded the initial estimate of around 425,000 DKr ($50,000), because of added expenses, changes in house plans during construction, inflation, and increased interest rates. In almost every built cohousing community, resale is no problem. In 1984, the first house put up for sale at Torn immediately sold for 780,000 DKr ($88,000), in an otherwise depressed housing market (up $21,000 from its original cost in 1976).

All six houses open on to the courtyard—the preferred outdoor sitting area even though most of the houses also have private patios in back.

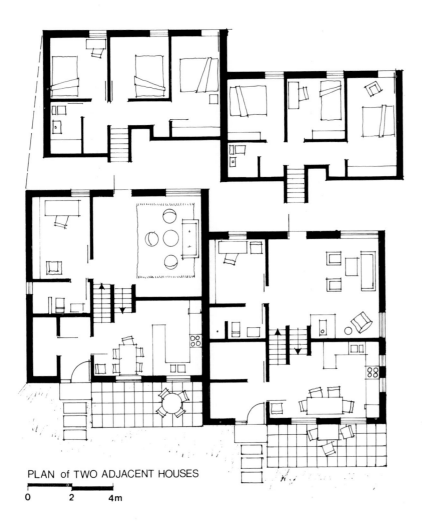

PLAN of TWO ADJACENT HOUSES

0   2   4m

Typical house floor plans.

and the fourth—perhaps most important—a cold beer. If the frustrated mechanic didn't manage to repair the car, at least he had a better time trying.

Over the years, the residents have renovated and restored the timber and mud structure that was formerly a farmhouse. Working weekends and holidays, they transformed the run-down two-story structure into a comfortable common house. In addition to the large kitchen and dining area, it also has a laundry room, children's playroom, workshop, storage room, music room, a cozy living room, and a guest room.

The common house has been particularly popular for music practice, especially with the teenagers. Soren, an accomplished drummer at 17, practices there a couple of hours each day without disturbing the rest of his family or neighbors. "As you get older," Soren explained, "you need a place like the old farmhouse to hang out in—not under the feet of your parents." His next-door neighbor added, "If he didn't have such a place, either his creativity or our peace of mind would be compromised."

Besides eating together twice a week, the community plans other joint activities about once a month—a trip to the zoo or the museum, hiking, swimming, a picnic, or just harvesting the apple trees. Holidays are often celebrated in the old farmhouse, where other friends and relatives can join in.

Tornevangsgarden shows how cohousing often results in development that helps preserve the historical and natural amenities of an area. Had the site been developed as apartments, or sectioned into typical single-family lots, the farmhouse (declared uninhabitable by county officials), the pond, and many of the old trees would have been lost. "The old farmhouse would have been torn down like all of the others that used to be in the area; it just wouldn't pay to keep it," said a resident.

Saturday at the Carport

As in every cohousing community, parking is kept to one side, using as little land as possible and keeping the living/playing area safer, cleaner, and quieter. At Torn, the residents built a carport after they moved in. Having all the cars in one place promotes casual interaction. One cold Saturday afternoon, as one resident labored under the hood of his malfunctioning auto, others chanced upon him on their way to and from their vehicles. The first offered a hand, the second advice, the third some better tools,

There are advantages and disadvantages to such a small cohousing community. We had thought that, as with a shared house, such close emotional quarters might encourage a high turnover rate. But after 12 years, only one household—a single father who found house payments difficult on only one income—has moved out. Even after moving, the father and his son still come back for common dinner one night a week.

According to the residents, several factors compensate for the close quarters. Several people knew each other before they undertook the project and shared similar intentions from the outset. The residents have also retained their relationships with other friends and neighbors. And because of its small scale, Torn doesn't plan as many common functions as larger cohousing communities do. Recently, in response to personal preferences, the number of common dinners was reduced from four to two a week.

While acknowledging the benefits of what they have built together, a number of residents expressed reservations about the small size of their community. "I don't think six families is the perfect number," said a father of two. "Maybe 20 is the right number. Six limits the level of activity, and if someone doesn't take part for a while you feel it. If someone doesn't do his share [common work days are about once a month], you notice it."

As in all cohousing communities, spontaneous socializing is just as meaningful as the planned activities. The beer-making club, for

The site plan illustrates how cohousing differs from typical development. The original site, A, could have been developed as single-family houses, B, which rarely foster community life, even if they utilize solar energy or incorporate beautiful aesthetics. Condominiums or apartments, C, attempt to emulate the privacy of single-family houses. The site plan which the residents chose, D, retains the site's assets for all six households to enjoy. 1. common house, 2. vegetable gardens, 3. pond, 4. carports.

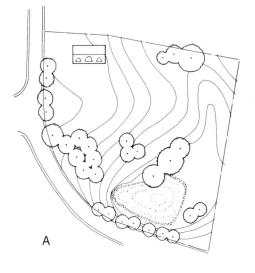

A

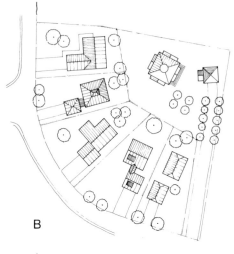

B

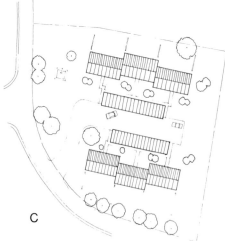

C

example, provides a number of unscheduled tasting parties. The courtyard scheme allows neighbors to meet casually as they come and go through the day. Kisse (a schoolteacher, mother, founding resident—and the woman Charles met back in 1980) describes the pleasure of spontaneous summer dinners in the courtyard:

> *Some days we'll just be working in our own vegetable gardens and someone will say, "Hey, I've got some potatoes," and another will add, "I've got some salad makings," and so on, until before you know it we have a potluck dinner in the courtyard and end up talking and drinking wine late into the night.*

> *Of course there are differences between the visions we had at the outset and the real thing. You can't really imagine what it will be like before you actually move in, and certainly all of our visions have not come true. Still, we wouldn't dream of moving out. It's practically heaven here, especially in the summer.*

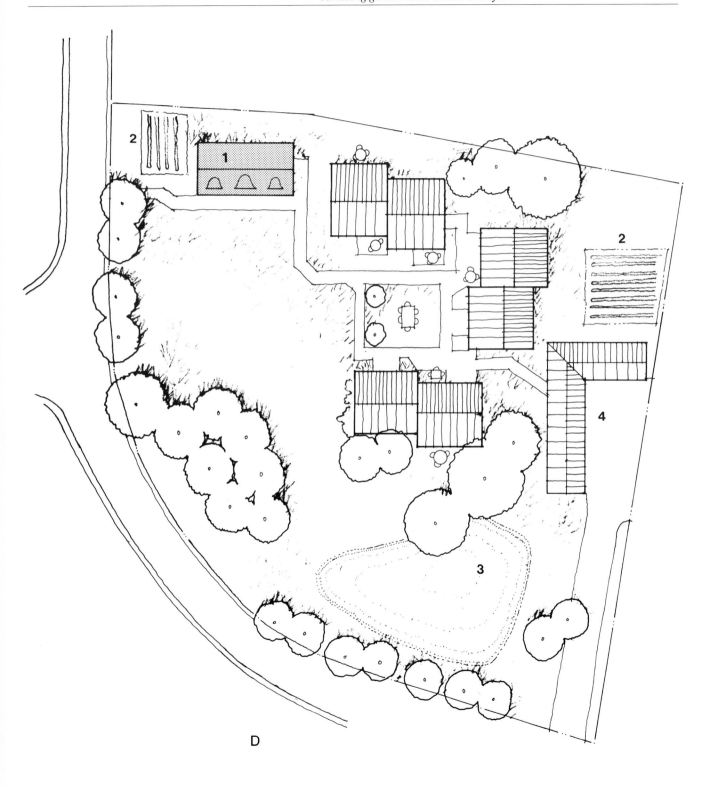

CHAPTER TEN

Skalbjerg, Denmark

20 Units

Architects:
Arkitektgruppen

Completed: 1978

Tenure: private and
rental

Common House:
5,100 ft² (474 m²)

Drejerbanken:
Half Owners, Half Renters

On Friday afternoon while some of the residents erected a huge tent, the children and teenagers built booths for tossing darts at balloons and other carnival games. Now, early on Saturday afternoon, folk instrumentalists circulate from house to house, enticing people out. By evening nearly two hundred guests and residents fill the tent —drinking, laughing, and feasting on the ox that has been roasting in an open pit all day. Vaudeville skits and musical performances follow the meal, with dancing and conversation continuing into the early hours of the morning. This is Drejerbanken's ninth annual summer festival. "It's an excuse to invite everyone you've wanted to see but haven't had the time to," a man shouts over the music.

Drejerbanken's Initial Organizing Agreement

• The organizing group will begin planning work with the current 25 adult members.

• New persons can join only if someone drops out; otherwise they will be put on the waiting list. Those on the waiting list can help with planning, but cannot vote.

• Membership entails an initial fee of 250 Dkr ($30), monthly dues of 100 Dkr ($11.50) up to a total of 2000 Dkr ($235), and agreement to assume planning responsibilities. The nonrefundable fees are to be spent on advertising, printing, and mailings. Any surplus will be used to furnish the common house.

• A "buddy system" will be utilized to welcome new members and explain the history and status of the group.

Drejerbanken is situated on the top of a clay hill (hence its name, "the potter's resource") in the small town of Skalbjerg. Though a farming town, Skalbjerg (population 400) is only 12 miles (18 km) west of Odense, the third largest city in Denmark —and the birthplace of poet and storyteller Hans Christian Andersen. Drejerbanken is the only Danish cohousing community to have both owner-occupied and rental nonprofit-owned residences—ten of each.

Defining the Dream

Drejerbanken's initiating group emerged from a seminar on housing alternatives for people who were reconsidering their housing situations. Participants from the seminar formed an organization called "Alternative Housing Types," whose purpose was to provide support and coordination for people who wished to develop a "local community," as cohousing was then called, "where there would be meaningful relationships among residents and where the future inhabitants would design and manage the dwellings and community buildings using direct democratic principles." Inspired by media articles about the inappropriateness of available housing options, and by an increasing awareness of new cohousing developments, they set out to improve their own residential situation.

The eight to ten founders advertised to reach others who might share their interests. Using flyers, radio announcements, public meetings and, most effectively, word of mouth, their group soon increased to 25 adults (7 singles and 9 couples). None had previous experience as planners, architects, or developers.

In April 1975 they established an initial organizing agreement. In retrospect, one resident recalls that there were only two criteria for joining the group: "First, to want to live in cohousing; and second, the desire to work for it." "Cohousers tend to be open-

minded and independent people," said another. "Open-minded enough to not merely accept what exists as the realm of possibilities, and independent enough to seek out what doesn't." Given the inevitable long meetings, patience and tolerance were also helpful traits. To avoid domination by a few individuals during the planning process, the group utilized a "round-table" discussion format in which each person could comment on a topic. "It was very successful," remembers a participant, "especially at incorporating new or shy members." Only when general consensus was not apparent did the group vote.

Inspired by several field trips to existing cohousing communities, the organizing group prepared a "wish list." Their proposal called for "a more balanced community, with a private life and a community life, a private garden and a common garden, a private dinner and a common dinner." One woman told us, "Community possibilities just aren't available in most neighborhoods. You have a private life at home and socialize with friends around the city, but you rarely have a community life near home. We felt that it adds to the quality of life and broadens the individual." They wanted a variety of ages—"to aid in fostering a renewed communication between the generations." They hoped to include a wide range of incomes, but realized that this might be a more difficult goal to attain, given that overall costs were as yet unknown. House prices needed to be as inexpensive as possible, at least below market rate, but they did not want to help with the construction themselves. They also wanted to be located near Odense, where most of them worked, and several people were interested in a large vegetable garden.

Having agreed on their intentions, the group refrained from further ideological debate and concentrated on finding a piece of property. By July 1975 they had located a

site owned by the county which was large enough for 20 dwellings. They optimistically hoped to start building in May 1976 and to move in by November 1976. But here they met their first setback: the county only finally agreed to sell them the land in November 1976. In retrospect, however, these extra months provided the additional time needed to organize a viable development proposal.

Not everyone in the group could afford private ownership, particularly the single parents. The membership approached a local nonprofit housing developer, saying, in effect: "You're in the business of developing low-income housing, and we're in the position of needing low-income units. Can we work together?"[1] The nonprofit housing organization had at that point developed

only 35 new rental units, but they accepted the challenge of developing housing with the future residents rather than for them.

Some residents of the town were dubious about the proposed development. Although the group held public meetings to familiarize neighbors with the project, they were still concerned about adding 50 people to a town of 400. "Nor was the county planning department particularly crazy about cohousing itself," recalls one participant. "It didn't fit neatly into their Master Plan."

When the group presented their project proposal to county officials in September 1975, it was rejected on the grounds that more than half of the units were rental. Feeling that this was just an excuse to reject the project itself, they appealed the decision.

Enjoying the afternoon with friends in front of the house.

Objectives of the Site Plan

- Ten owner-occupied and ten rental houses

- One common house, 3,230 to 4,305 ft² (300 to 400 m²)

- 32 parking spaces located at the site periphery

- Divided into two parcels: rental and owner-occupied (as required by the Ministry of Housing in order for the nonprofit-owned rental units to qualify for subsidies)

- Common outdoor sitting and recreational areas

- Common gardens and private gardens

- Common house visible from private dwellings

- Optimum solar exposure

- Relatively short distance from each house to common house

Remembers one woman:

We all showed up at the appeal hearing, and all we had to ask was "Why not?" They couldn't answer. Basically the planning commissioners realized that they were just suspicious of the unknown. But when they looked at us, they could see that we were people very much like themselves. They had to ask themselves, "What real reason do we have to deny them?" They could not refuse us.

The county approved the project with the stipulation that only ten units be rental, and in the end the local authorities proved very supportive. The group proceeded with the design of ten owner-occupied units and ten rental units.

The Design Process
The design process was highly interactive. The design firm, Arkitektgruppen, participated in group meetings, helped coordinate weekend sessions and field trips, and guided the group through the complex development process. They began with the site plan.

Using blocks to represent the residences and working in small groups, the participants developed 25 potential site plans (12 more or less identical). Three schemes that best conformed to the goals were selected for further development by the architects.

The House Designs. In a "house game" devised by the architects, residents arranged room, furniture, and stair cut-outs onto modules to generate house plans. Because the rental houses were subject to more restrictions and therefore a longer review process, the group began by designing them first according to the following objectives:

- Compact and inexpensive
- Simple geometry, consistent construction techniques
- Medium-sized bedrooms, small living spaces

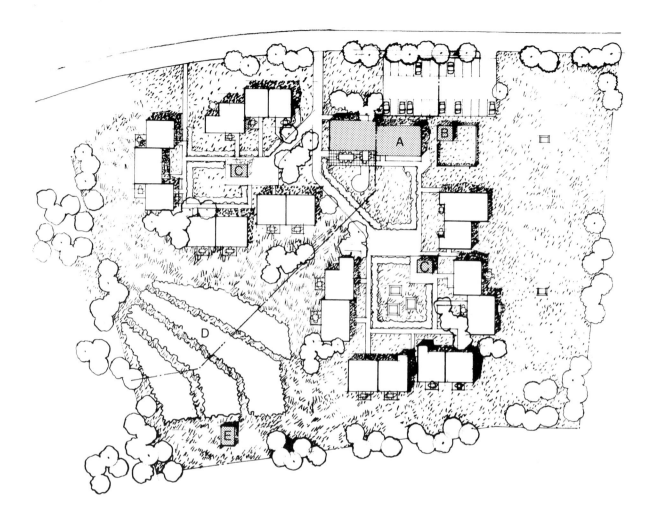

Site plan: A. common house, B. furnace building, C. storage shed, D. vegetable garden, E. chicken house.

- Good exposure and accessibility between outdoors and indoors
- Large kitchens oriented toward the front of the house
- Natural materials
- Living spaces oriented toward rear of house and private gardens
- Standardization of kitchens and bathrooms
- Bedrooms off of living areas
- Minimal hallways
- Possibility of installing solar panels at a later date
- Possibility for later additions

Unfortunately, because they were building publicly assisted rental housing only limited experimentation in design was permitted (no use of renewable energy, for example). How much the cohousers could deviate from government requirements was entirely up to the good will of the bureaucrats. The process was a little easier, however, because the future residents themselves were making the requests. For example, the Ministry of Housing wanted the common house divided, one-half for renters and another half for owners, separated by a fire wall, while the residents wanted it complete-

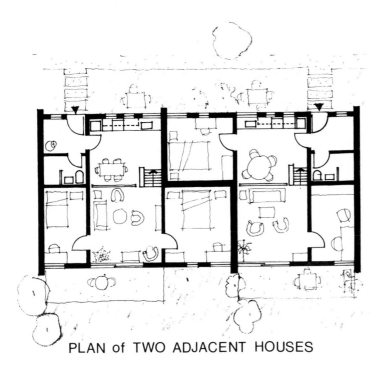

PLAN of TWO ADJACENT HOUSES

Two of the smaller rental houses.

ly open, with no distinction between the two halves. After lengthy discussion the residents were allowed to go ahead with their design.

The designs of the rental units were considered so successful that the prospective owners decided to use the same construction standards and development cost per square foot, with the size dependent on how much the household was willing to pay. They agreed on five private house plans and five rental house plans, with slight variations, such as partitioning the living room to create a study. The construction bids were favorable, but cost reductions were still required. Interior wood sheathing, some plumbing fixtures, and closets were cut back and/or replaced with less expensive materials.

Reassessing the Development Process
Discouragement was a major obstacle. With continuing delays, no one knew exactly when they would move in; how many meetings, hearings, and years would it take? The

building and planning officials' unfamiliarity with cohousing made getting the necessary approvals especially difficult. The design and budget of the rental portion also had to be reviewed by the nonprofit developer and the Ministry of Housing.

From the time the development group agreed on the site in September 1975, until June of 1978 when residents started moving in, 73 adults actively participated in the development process. Some people left and rejoined the group at a later date. Reasons for dropping out ranged from job or family changes and economic considerations, to ideological or personality conflicts and sheer impatience. Turnover caused old questions to reappear, calling for a reestablishment of the group's exact intentions and status. In the final stages, delays also arose from the group's lack of building experience. Of course, the combination of rental and owner-occupied units made the process more complicated.

Drejerbanken Today
Located at the northern corner, the common house forms the focus of the development's layout. The 20 houses are oriented around two courtyards, both of which embrace the common house.

The common house is the development's hub. One passes it when walking from the parking area to the individual houses, and it can be seen from the front yard of every dwelling. The one- and two-story attached houses are grouped in two clusters, one of rental and one of owner-occupied dwellings (as required by the Ministry of Housing), each situated around a courtyard. Clustering the houses preserved space for a soccer field, common garden and wooded "fantasy area" where the children play.

The buildings are constructed simply and consistently, in terms of both construction materials and building forms. All house plans have the same core design for kitchen, dining room, living room, bathroom, and entry; the bedrooms are added either vertically or horizontally. The rental houses range in size from 765 to 1,100 square feet (71–102 m²), owner-occupied houses from 845 to 1,370 square feet (79–128 m²).[2]

Although officially only 2,550 square feet (237 m²), the common house has a full basement, effectively doubling its size to 5,100 square feet (474 m²). Its facilities include a dining/meeting room; a kitchen, pantry, and scullery; a reading room; two children's playrooms; and a large vestibule where the

mailboxes are located. One resident set up her pottery studio in the common house in exchange for some of her wares. The basement houses a workshop, storage space, a laundry room with two large washers and one dryer, and a yet-to-be-completed sauna.

The Residents. Twenty-four children and 28 adults (18 women and 10 men) live in Drejerbanken. Of the twenty households, seven are couples, eleven are single parents, and two are singles. Drejerbanken was the first project in which the majority of the residents were single parents, primarily because

Development Timeline

Nov 74	First meeting.
Apr 75	Organizing agreement established.
Jul 75	Site selected. Architect and attorney hired.
Aug 75	Schematic design presented to county.
Sep 75	Proposal approved. Nonprofit agrees to sponsor rental units.
Nov 75	Site plan finalized. Begin house designs.
Jan 76	Nonprofit purchases site for rental units.
Mar 76	Preliminary design of rentals and common house.
Apr 76	Preliminary design of private houses.
May 76	7 households buy remaining half of site.
Jun 76	Design for rental units and common house sent to Ministry of Housing for approval.
Feb 77	Ministry approves rentals and proposes new timeline.
Apr 77	Design of private units completed. Last 3 houses sold.
May 77	Begin working drawings.
Oct 77	Construction begins.
Jul 78	All rental units occupied.
Oct 78	Construction & landscaping completed. All houses occupied.

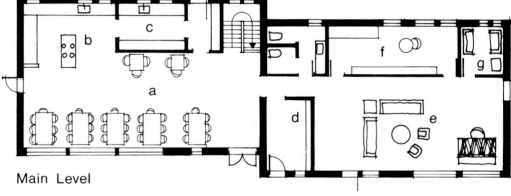

Main Level

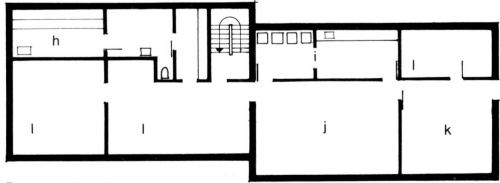

Basement Level

Common house floor plan: a. dining room, b. kitchen, c. scullery, d. entry and mailboxes, e. sitting/crafts room, f. pottery studio, g. youth room, h. sauna, i. laundry, j. drying room, k. workshop, l. storage.

Residents relax in the common house after dinner.

Work Groups

Budgeting (and bookkeeping): two adults, two years

Dinner (budgeting and purchasing): two adults, one year

Energy (and energy-conservation): three adults, time varies.

Culture (parties, films, lectures and outings): participation varies.

Chicken Duty: two adults for 14 days

of the rental option. The mixed tenure allows people to move from renter to owner, which has been done, and from owner to renter, which has not yet been done.

Management. Renters and owners manage Drejerbanken together. Resident meetings, held every two weeks, are the forum for making community decisions. Usually the residents reach conclusions by consensus, but they occasionally resort to voting. Owners and renters sometimes have separate meetings—for example, when the renters discuss an upcoming report for the nonprofit organization or the owners discuss new property tax laws—but not for issues of mutual concern.

Financial decisions require more time for consideration, and are rarely decided at one meeting. If any expense exceeds 500 Dkr ($58), an individual may choose not to contribute. Monthly contributions toward maintenance and community purchases are proportional to the size of each house, averaging 520 Dkr ($60) per month. Besides maintenance, this money is used for repairs (e.g., washing machines); purchases (e.g., a new oven). Cultural activities and yearly work projects are financed separately.

Organization. "Before we moved in, we thought that everything would run smoothly by virtue of everyone's good intentions," a resident once wrote. He continued:

Predictably, soon afterward we learned the reality of getting things done. Therefore, rather than just assigning duties we sought imaginative ways of accomplishing tasks. For example, five separate groups tend the five sections of the common vegetable garden. Participation is voluntary, but if you don't volunteer, you're drafted. The person who volunteers to be "in charge" of the section that grows the carrots and potatoes officially doesn't have to do any of the work, but must coordinate the effort.

In fact, residents do most of the work together. "But the problem is that everyone wants to volunteer to be in charge," one woman joked. Chores are done by small work groups, with each adult participating in at least one for a specific period of time, and with the children also involved.

Dinner is prepared every night in the common house. Participation varies; in the 12 evenings we were there, 38 to 46 of the 54 residents attended. Each night three adults and two children make dinner and clean up afterward. Each adult cooks three times a month, and each child helps twice a month, starting at age seven. The meal cost is fixed at 10 Dkr ($1.20) per adult, and half price for children.

Saturday mornings are reserved for general common house clean-up, with mandatory participation at least once every four weeks. Brunch often follows the morning chores. Four to six work days per year are devoted to less glamorous tasks—purging storage rooms of clutter, miscellaneous landscaping chores, chicken coop scrubdown, and window washing. These jobs are performed on a purely voluntary basis, according to one's personal proclivities. The high level of volunteerism for unpopular chores is an excellent demonstration of Drejerbanken's success in promoting community spirit. As with

other work projects, all of these shared tasks contribute to the intergenerational cooperation that these cohousers advocate.

In addition to the work days, the community takes on one major project each year. One year they remodeled the common house, changing partitions and adding acoustic ceiling panels. Another year they built a fancy chicken house. The summer we were there they were remodeling the common kitchen. "The annual project each year helps maintain some of that positive cooperative energy we had when we were planning Drejerbanken," one resident told us.

Evaluation Week. Once a year, when the winter evenings are long, Drejerbanken has "evaluation week." Everyone sets aside a couple of evenings and the following weekend to "air out the sheets." The discussion ranges from practical organization to social activities, from children's concerns to next year's projects. This provides the opportunity to go beyond routine business to explore what might make Drejerbanken even better.

The evaluation process begins with two discussion evenings, where the community breaks into four groups of six to seven adults each. The smaller meetings allow people to express themselves more effectively and without intimidation. One woman explained:

You learn a great deal about yourself in these meetings. When someone asks how you feel about this or that, then you have to ask yourself, "Well, how do I feel?"

The topics that arise become the platform for the larger discussion. The children, divided by age into three groups, hold separate meetings. The adults provide the young people with questions to discuss amongst themselves, and they may add to the list as they wish. After setting the agenda, the whole

Illustrating the virtues of cooperation, one woman cleans up after dinner, while other residents relax without guilt, knowing their turn will come another evening.

group spends an intensive weekend discussing topics.

The evaluation process facilitates communication, allowing differences to be heard and misunderstandings to dissipate. "People are more candid with each other for months afterward," remarked one resident. At the week's end—after all have discussed their points of view—the whole community holds a "winter fest."

A Successful Model of Diversity

Drejerbanken has successfully combined owner-occupied and rental units, encompassing a diversity of incomes and households. "We're surprised that more cohousing groups haven't done it," remarked one woman. Even their accountant admits how difficult it was to keep the books straight—a job that has now been computerized.

Several owner/renter myths have been dispelled at Drejerbanken. The first is that renters are less stable and have a higher turnover than owners. Since 1978, three owners and only two renters have moved out of Drejerbanken. Another myth is that owners take better care of their homes and gardens than renters. Yet, the prize for the best roses goes to a renter; otherwise the homes and yards are indistinguishable. A third myth is that having rental units slows the appreciation rate of the owner-occupied houses. Cohousing dwellings typically appreciate faster than comparable houses, and Drejerbanken is no exception.

When Drejerbanken was built, public officials were unsure that owners and renters could "manage" in the same project. As it turns out, renters and owners are equally involved in all aspects of management, and visitors cannot distinguish who rents and who owns, although social scientists have come from throughout Europe to study the phenomenon. This underscores Drejerbanken's success at including a truly diverse combination of residents.

An Interview with Niels Revsgaard

During our 14-day visit to Drejerbanken, we stayed with Niels Revsgaard, a bachelor and senior lecturer in sociology at the Odense Teachers Training College. Niels has given much consideration to communities—from the kibbutzim of Israel to rural villages and urban cooperatives closer to home, and specifically for the last nine years as a cohousing resident. While at Drejerbanken we talked with Niels about cohousing and about his community.

Charles: What do you think about living in cohousing? Who do you think chooses this lifestyle?

Niels: I think that it's a much more balanced way to live. Living alone, or in a contemporary nuclear family, people have lots of privacy, but often not as much community life as they want or need. In fact, I think that some people forget or even deny how important community life is.

In the past, many cohousing residents, and certainly the founders, were relatively well educated and forward thinking. But today people choose cohousing because it's pragmatic, because of the children (whether they are yours or not), and for personal growth. Today all kinds of people move into cohousing—it's becoming mainstream. One resident now living here came to visit a friend one day and said to herself right then that she wanted to live here. She had never even considered cohousing before.

Charles: As a bachelor, why did you choose to live here?

Niels: To have more contact with children and families, with a more varied group of people than I would otherwise associate with. I get to know children of all ages without having to have my own. Typically bachelors associate with people they know from work, or people with whom they share very similar lifestyles. Bachelors tend to live in a "singles" world. Living here, I spend time with people I normally would not. It's also convenient for a bachelor, as it is for everyone. I help prepare dinner only three times a month, but eat extremely well the rest of the time.

Charles: How do you think that living in cohousing influences an individual?

Niels: A person can do more than they would ordinarily on their own. Living in cohousing broadens people by getting them to do things they might not have otherwise tried. You see someone cross-country skiing out in the yard, and think "Hey, if he can do that, then I probably can too." In addition, the owner of the skis probably wouldn't mind lending them to you (along with a few words of advice) so that you can give it a try. Another example is playing musical instruments. People typically play music if they happen to have had some exposure to it in their youth. At Drejerbanken all of the children are exposed to the few adults who play music, and as a result almost all of them play some instrument.

One criticism could be that there can be pressure to do things in cohousing. Some people who hadn't previously gone abroad for their vacations might feel some pressure to do so now, when their neighbors talk about their trips so much. But I feel that it's more of a positive influence than a pressure. In general I feel that living in cohousing fosters independence and maturity—you learn to cooperate on a small scale, and to accomplish more as an individual.

People get to know you as a whole person in cohousing. In many ways modern society is schizophrenic. You show one side of yourself at work and another side at home; you may begin to wonder who you are. We don't demonstrate an integrated personality, a functional and emotional side; in fact, you don't even get a chance to develop an integrated personality. Cohousing can also give you a sense of reference as an individual; because people ask your opinion, you have to try and find one and in so doing learn who you are.

I would also emphasize that living in cohousing produces a set of valuable experiences that can be used in professional life. The acquired ability to cooperate is obvious; common meetings go much more smoothly and quickly than they initially did. A broader range of experiences and more highly developed social skills have been very relevant to my teaching; I've had more contacts and more opportunity to develop ideas. Furthermore, I think I have more professional opportunities living here than I would if I lived elsewhere.

Charles: As a sociologist, how do you think living in cohousing affects the family?

Niels: It takes a lot of pressure off the family. In general, the modern marriage is overstressed, especially emotionally. The attitudes of men and women are changing, but not harmoniously. Thirty years ago, sex roles were defined for the most part. Perhaps in 20 years those roles will have settled into their new patterns, but in the meantime changes create tension and stress. A cohousing environment balances marriage and offers some relief to the emotional burdens on the modern family. Living in a community provides an inherent support system—not just someone to talk to, but also pleasant distractions from the pressures of contemporary life.

Charles: While living in San Francisco, one of us often has to work late, leaving

the other without someone to share the day's traumas, glories, or dinner with. At Trudeslund (our residence for six months), if one of us was late, the other was usually found in the common house engrossed in after-dinner conversation, with the other's absence hardly detected.

Niels: Some might see that as a problem. For example, divorce in cohousing might seem easier than it otherwise is, because an estranged spouse can see that they can live without their partner—they have others for companionship. People who live in today's small nuclear families have to ask themselves twice, "What will I do without him (or her)? Who else would I have?" A mother with two children who desires a divorce must carefully consider the dramatic lifestyle consequences. Will she be able to remain in the family home? Will she be lonely? Will it be too difficult to raise the children alone? Obviously, cohousing doesn't eliminate these problems, nor should it try to, but it does add to people's independence. They don't need a partner just for company! Yet, even though divorce might appear easier in cohousing, the statistics show that the divorce rate for people who live in cohousing is lower than for comparable segments of the general population.

Today there is often a lot of strife in traditional houses over domestic chores; is everyone doing their share? Domestic responsibilities are divided more equally among the adults here, so *he* has to cook as often as she does, at least communally.

Charles: Back in California, Kathryn and I had agreed to rotate cooking, but somehow she ended up cooking both more frequent and more savory dinners. Yet, I loved to cook at Trudeslund. What's the difference?

Niels: Men like to cook when they can get recognition, like at your American barbecues. They usually do like to cook in cohousing. They receive acknowledgment for a "job well done," and from more than just the family. The camaraderie among the people preparing dinner not only makes it fun, but also helps prevent disaster. Perhaps even more relevant is that almost everyone here, men and women, shuffles papers all day without really producing anything. Common dinners give everyone an opportunity to actually produce something.

Charles: How do children feel about Drejerbanken?

Niels: You should ask them. We do, and they usually seem positive. I feel there are favorable conditions for children here—socially, physically, and educationally. They are exposed to many more interests and stimulations than usual—participating in meetings and learning to work cooperatively, for example.

They also have a strong sense of identity. They are not anonymous here; and like the children of any village, they know that there is a place they are recognized and have a sense of belonging. This enhances their self-confidence. Children who live in cohousing are usually "can do" people because they learn from participating in so many kinds of activities, and receive recognition for their accomplishment. The child who plays the guitar is known for that, the skier is known because he skis—it becomes part of his identity.

Charles: What about the work projects?

Niels: The most important thing about the work weekends, the yearly work projects, the garden work, and other activities is that they give us an excuse to do something together. A project gives everyone something in common again, something to talk about.

The work projects are also great for the children. They get to know and work with adults other than their parents, and learn to communicate with adults. Without the projects, children might not have anything to talk to adults about; dialogue might never get started. At the same time, the projects give them a sense of worthiness and acknowledgment beyond the usual, "Now, whose kid are you?"

Charles: What about decision making?

Niels: One person, one vote. It should be as democratic as possible, even if it requires lengthy discussion. Children vote on issues concerning them. It can make a child feel "ten feet tall" to participate in meetings. It's best not to delegate decision making. Someone operating on implied authority makes me nervous—we have enough of that in our lives. Here we can practice direct democracy, so why not? If people feel left out of decisions, they become frus-

trated and move out of the decision-making process, or even worse, the community.

Charles: What is Drejerbanken's relationship with Skalbjerg?

Niels: The important distinction is that the residents of Drejerbanken are urbanites who work and thrive in the city of Odense, but live in a small town. We have to be conscious of the divergent value systems if we don't want to alienate our neighbors. For example, we are careful not to wield our disproportionate influence in a provoking manner (which would be relatively easy to do because we are inherently organized.) If we share an opinion about a certain issue facing the school board, we don't show up at the meeting *en masse*. We are usually better informed on topics than most people, however, because before a town meeting we will probably discuss the topic here. But we rarely vote or act as a whole; we are just as likely to disagree with each other as with anyone else.

I have heard that most people in

Skalbjerg recognize Drejerbanken as an asset to the town. The common house is used for everything from town meetings to music practice—with or without residents of Drejerbanken. We have a soccer field that children from the whole town use, and they're almost always assured of someone else to play with.

Charles: What do you think about the owner/renter mixture at Drejerbanken?

Niels: We make very little of it really, especially compared to all of the Europeans who come to "study" it. On occasion we do need to be sensitive to our mixed tenure. We don't locate common tables in the two courtyards. That might begin to separate us, if not now (given how well we know each other) then perhaps later, when there might be more turnover. Instead, we put tables up near the common house. The owner/renter mixture is a good idea for all the obvious reasons. I really appreciate it. But it does make the financing and planning a bit more complicated.

Notes
1. Nonprofit housing developers utilize special financing available through the Danish government (typically subsidizing about 20 percent of the development cost) to build rental housing, which is then owned and managed by the nonprofit.
2. Government regulations dictated that the rental units average 1,025 ft^2 (95 m^2) to qualify for financing as nonprofit rentals. The residents, however, chose to contribute 10 m^2 of each rental unit to the common house, so their actual average size is 915 ft^2 (85 m^2). The owner-occupied houses average 1,163 ft^2 (108 m^2) including 10.5 m^2 of the common house, and therefore they actually average 1,050 ft^2 (98 m^2). Nonprofit housing projects typically allow 3 percent of the building area for common facilities. Three percent of 950 square meters equals 29 square meters (307 ft^2). Therefore the common house is 237 square meters (2,551 ft^2) total.

Children play in front of one of Bondbjerget's four common houses which each have a kitchen and dining room, living room, children's playroom, workshop, and crafts room. Although all 80 units are rentals, the complex was initiated, planned and is now managed by the residents similarly to owner-occupied cohousing developments.

CHAPTER ELEVEN

Odense, Denmark

80 units

Architects:
Faellestegnestuen;
Sten Holbaek,
Erik Christiansen, and
Frede Nielsen

Built: 1982–83

Tenure: rental

Common Houses:
four at 3,875 ft² each
(360 m²)

Bondebjerget:
Four in One

This small group of residents from a 500-unit government-subsidized housing project knew what they wanted: to develop a housing complex that would emphasize community and that would involve the residents both in the planning and ongoing management. Dissatisfied with the social isolation and health problems of the 1960s block housing they lived in, the group took their proposal to the nonprofit housing organization that managed their complex. Several members of the group were familiar with cohousing, and one had been involved in the planning of the nearby Drejerbanken community. At the time they organized, cohousing was generally privately financed, and these residents could not afford that option. During their first meeting in December 1979, the residents asked the Odense Cooperative Housing Association (OCHA) to work with them to build a rental cohousing community. To their surprise, the association was not only receptive, but it already had a policy to support the development of cohousing.

The private dwellings are oriented around four courtyards to maintain the intimate scale residents desired.

Cooperative housing associations in Denmark are nonprofit organizations whose function is to develop and manage subsidized rental housing. In the 1970s, housing associations had begun to recognize the benefits of resident participation in planning and managing buildings, especially in reducing maintenance problems and vandalism. Despite increased resident involvement, however, housing associations continued to control most development decisions. OCHA knew that if the cohousing experiment was to succeed, the organization's role must be restricted to overseeing the project's financial and administrative plan. OCHA therefore accepted the group's proposal that the residents themselves determine the program and choose the site and the architect.

The organizing group's initial goal was to develop a community of 20 to 30 units, but when they found a large site that fit their other criteria, they worked out a plan for four groups of 20 units each. While OCHA handled the red tape involved in acquiring the site and financing the project, the resident group visited existing cohousing communities, clarified its goals, and interviewed architects. A brochure describing the proposed community was distributed at local libraries and other public facilities to attract other participants.

After some debate, the residents convinced OCHA to accept their choice of architect, even though he had less experience in housing than the others they had considered. Through his background in hospital design, architect Sten Holbaek had considerable experience with participatory design processes. From the earliest discussions about what residents desired, Holbaek

Bondebjerget site plan:
1. common house, 2. parking,
3. playground.

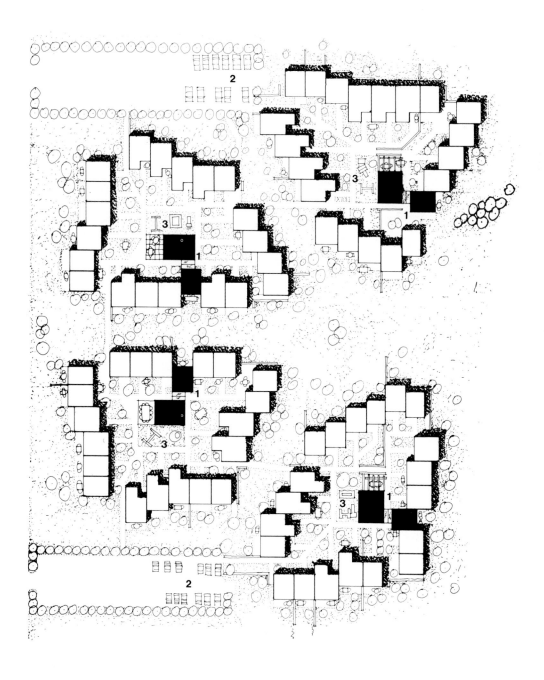

Common house floor plan.

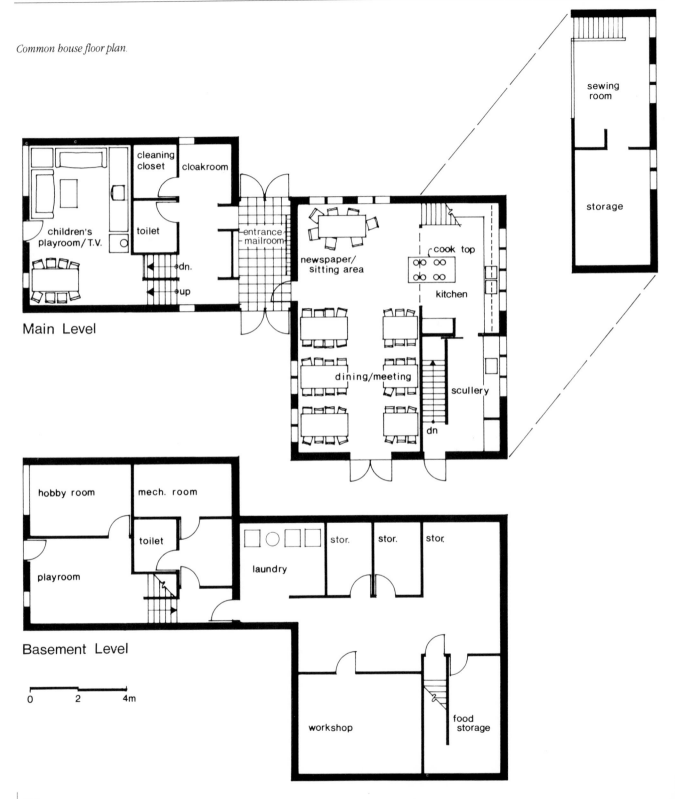

Main Level

Basement Level

0   2   4m

brought up many new considerations. In assessing sample site plans, residents learned to articulate their opinions about the relationship between community and private areas. Holbaek involved residents in the entire design process, even meeting with individual households to discuss their specific requirements. Looking back on the design phase, several residents credited the architect with helping them through the most difficult stages when they were considering abandoning the project.

The Four Clusters

Although the four clusters at Bondebjerget (which means "the farmer's hill") have almost identical common facilities, each has its own personality. Group One's residents were the most involved in the planning process and include the project's initiators, so they know each other and the development's history better than do the other clusters. Only one family from Group One moved out during the first three years of occupancy, and the reason was job related. Common dinners are available three to four times a week, averaging 40 participants (75 percent) on any given evening.

Group Two moved in two months after Group One, but only a few people were acquainted with each other beforehand. Having missed the planning process, these residents had differing expectations, which resulted in several years of instability. At the time of our visit, two and a half years later, there were two distinct cliques and some resentment among residents. Nevertheless, the common house is well used and dinners are available three to four nights a week. Several households had moved out, and relationships seemed to be improving. Without the positive example and support of the other three clusters, this group might have given up altogether.

Although residents of the third cluster did

not participate in the planning process, most of them had worked together in a local political organization before moving in. This shared experience made their transition to cohousing relatively easy. Group Three is now the most active cluster; all residents participate in the common dinners, which are available every night of the week.

The common house kitchen and dining room of Group One.

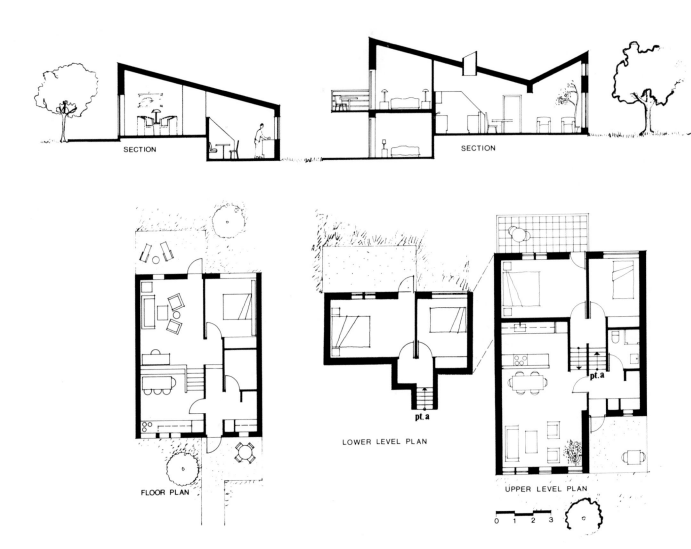

SECTION

SECTION

FLOOR PLAN

LOWER LEVEL PLAN

pt. a

UPPER LEVEL PLAN

pt. a

0   1   2   3

*One-bedroom, 625 ft² (58 m²),
and four-bedroom, 1,205 ft²
(112 m²), units.*

The interior of Bondebjerget's private dwellings show that inexpensive housing can also be quite beautiful.

Group Four was the last to move in, eight months after the first, and they too did not know each other beforehand. Acknowledging that it has taken time to get acquainted, they are generally pleased with the community. "We don't dismiss each other's ideas or opinions—our attitude is let's try it," explained one resident. Several households moved in without understanding the cohousing concept and found it was not for them. Having survived this turnover, an adjustment period of getting to know each other, and trials of various organizational systems, Group Four is settling in.

The experiences of the four groups illustrate the importance of the planning process in clarifying residents' expectations and developing open communication. When residents move in without knowing each other, their ability to work together is a matter of chance. Sometimes it works, as for Group Four, and other times it is more difficult, as Group Two found. The strength of Bondebjerget's initiating group was undoubtedly the key to the success of the community as a whole. It will be interesting to see how each of the groups develops over time.

Management, Maintenance, and Common Activities

Initially residents had complete control of the waiting list for available units. After the

community is the wide range of activities made possible. The Cultural Committee organizes a monthly film club, theater classes for children, special lectures, and musical events. The Buying Association allows residents to purchase many items at a discount. Bondebjerget is also directly across from a school that many of the children attend and whose facilities they can use.

A Mutually Beneficial Partnership

As nonprofit-owned rentals, the community is open to all income levels, allowing for considerable resident diversity. Of the 20 households in Group One, seven are single parents, four are singles without children at home, and nine are couples with children. Individual rent subsidies are available according to household income.

As a partnership between a resident group and a nonprofit housing organization, this community has taken advantage of the strengths of each. By allowing the residents to control the development process, OCHA has minimized its management and maintenance efforts. Even with the difficulties some of the groups had initially, the residents have taken responsibility for all daily management. The organization oversees rent collection and long-range financial matters, minimizing the financial risks of residents. A development of this size would be almost impossible without the involvement of an experienced developer; by contrast, the largest owner-occupied Danish cohousing development is 36 units.

In our week at Bondebjerget, we were struck by similarities between it and the entirely owner-occupied cohousing communities we had visited. The degree of resident involvement, the types of common activities, and the interaction between neighbors were all very similar. The primary difference is the relatively low monthly cost, and who can therefore afford to live there.

After retiring from teaching, Sigrid decided to move to Bondebjerget because she was not "going to just sit in that house alone and get older." Here she has complete autonomy and a community just outside her door.

second year of occupancy, they decided to relinquish this responsibility to OCHA, which offers openings to the next persons on the waiting list in the traditional manner. "We want it to be open to everyone and not to become a special group," explained Sos, who has been involved since the very beginning. Residents have made up a new brochure to ensure that potential residents know what to expect.

Each cluster is responsible for organizing its own common activities. Common meetings for the entire development are held every other month, and a coordinating committee, made up of one representative from each group and a chairperson, oversees daily management. Four percent of the development's annual budget is allocated for common activities (approximately 100,000 DKr or $12,500). Decisions on how monies are used require a majority vote by the common meeting. A maintenance committee with two representatives from each group takes care of general maintenance, with community-wide "work weekends" planned four times a year.

One of the advantages of such a large

PART THREE

Creating Cohousing

*W*hen we compare the approaches that different cohousing groups have taken, it is obvious that some methods work better than others. The following chapters examine the cohousing development process in detail, how it has evolved, and the consequences of different strategies and solutions. Based on 20 years of Danish experience, this analysis provides a solid background for exploring appropriate applications of cohousing in the United States.

The 33-unit Skraplanet development, initiated and designed by Jan Gudmand-Høyer, was one of the first Danish cohousing communities. Although considered conservative by today's standards, it established the concepts on which later cohousing communities have built.

CHAPTER TWELVE

As more people move into cohousing communities, more people —friends, neighbors, and relatives—find out what this way of living is all about and see its advantages. Then they want to try it themselves.

Hans S. Andersen

The Evolution of Cohousing

The first attempt to build what the Danes know today as *bofællesskaber* began in the winter of 1964 when Danish architect Jan Gudmand-Høyer gathered a group of friends to discuss current housing options. Contemplating starting a family, Gudmand-Høyer and his wife, a psychologist, were tired of living in the city, which at the time seemed caught in a downward spiral of disintegration. They agreed with their friends that neither the single-family suburban house nor the multi-story apartment building offered a desirable alternative. Row houses were less isolating than other forms of housing, but they lacked the common facilities that provide a true sense of community.

Over several months, this circle of friends discussed possibilities for a more supportive living environment. They sought the qualities of a country village, but a location near the city with its professional and cultural opportunities. Agreeing that cooperation was as necessary at home as in the workplace, they decided their housing complex should be small enough to allow residents to know each other and to feel comfortable using the common area as an extended living room. In addition, the design should encourage social interaction between neighbors; and, most importantly, "a housing program should not be carried out for people, but by people."[2]

Among their sources of inspiration was Thomas More's book, *Utopia*, written in 1516. More describes a city of cooperatives, each consisting of 30 families who share common facilities and meals, and who organize child care and other practical functions.

Danish projects, such as the Doctors' Association Housing built in Copenhagen in 1853, also provided inspiration. These workers' row houses were primarily designed to provide healthful light and air to every dwelling, but their intimate scale also encouraged active community life in the complex. In the late 1800s and early 1900s, workers took the initiative themselves to develop better housing with the founding of

the Workers' Building Association. A popular Danish novel about a working-class boy, *Pelle Erobreren* (Pelle the Conqueror) by Martin Andersen Nexo, describes this cooperative building movement and has kept alive the idea of people organizing to improve their housing situation.

By the end of 1964, Gudmand-Høyer's group was ready to put its ideas into action. Fully expecting to occupy their new housing community within a few years, they bought a site in the quiet town of Hareskov on the outskirts of Copenhagen, and developed plans for 12 terraced houses set around a common house and swimming pool.

Gudmand-Høyer's design for Hareskov is relatively conservative in comparison to cohousing developments built today. Individual residences were quite large and very private, with walls enclosing entrances and backyards. Experience has shown that privacy is not as important as casual interaction between private dwellings and common areas. The Hareskov design de-emphasizes the common house, which is hidden from public view under a central plaza; by contrast, the common house is a prominent feature of cohousing developments today.

Despite Gudmand-Høyer's careful, conservative approach, the Hareskov proposal met with mixed reactions. Local officials supported the proposal, but the neighbors did not. Gudmand-Høyer wrote later:

We had not anticipated the reaction of the neighbors. Even though we had very neutrally called the development Skovbakken [Forest Hill], and even though we had not used the word "collective" in our description . . . they simply saw "red."

The neighbors officially opposed the project on the grounds that the increased number of children would bring excessive noise to their quiet neighborhood. They organized

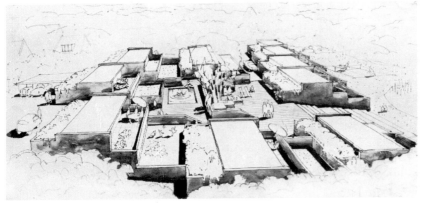

The Hareskov project, designed by Jan Gudmand-Høyer, consisted of 12 houses around a common house.

and bought the property needed for access to the group's building site. After a year of trying to work out an agreement with the Hareskov neighbors, the group was finally forced to sell the site. Discouraged by this ordeal, most of the families gave up.

During the ensuing period of reflection, Gudmand-Høyer wrote an article entitled "The Missing Link Between Utopia and the Dated One-Family House," in which he described his group's ideas and the Hareskov project. When published in a national newspaper in 1968, it elicited a tremendous response. In the following months, Gudmand-Høyer received letters and phone calls from more than one hundred people interested in living in a place like the one he described. There was suddenly interest "to build not only one community, but three or four."[3]

Changing Attitudes

In the four years since Gudmand-Høyer had first gathered his friends to discuss housing alternatives, Western societies had begun to experience a drastic shift in values. By 1968, the youth movement was exploding in Europe and the United States, with student uprisings at many major universities, including those in Berkeley, Paris, and Copenhagen. Many people not directly involved in the protests were influenced by the spirit of the day and began questioning conventional measures of success. This shift in attitude, supported by a belief that a more cooperative living environment would help build a more humane world, fueled attempts to create new ways of living together.

Collectives (or shared houses), where people share a house or apartment, became a popular housing option among young people. Larger collectives or communes, often based on radical political and social ideals, new family structures, or Eastern religions, sprouted throughout North America

Children drop in on their neighbors in search of playmates in this cohousing community.

and Europe. For most couples with children, collectives were not a realistic long-term option, but the cooperative lifestyle of the emerging cohousing concept promised greater support for the needs of the nuclear family.

In addition to Gudmand-Høyer, others were writing about the cohousing concept. In 1967, author Bodil Graae published an article entitled "Children Should Have One Hundred Parents," in which she argues that children's needs are not provided for in modern society—that neighborhood design gives greater consideration to cars and parking than to children, and that most of society considers children an unwelcome nuisance. Graae envisions an environment where children can "go in and out of the homes around us. . . crawl under hedges. . . feel like they belong." In such a community all the adults would look after all the children. She asked people interested in "a housing collective with the common denominator 'also for children'" to contact her. Over fifty people responded, and a group began meeting regularly to discuss how to build such a place.

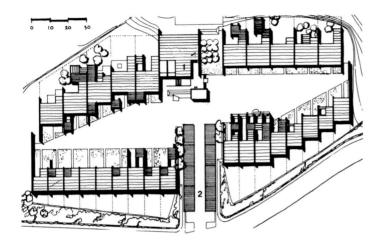

Saettedammen site plan: 1. common house, 2. parking.

The articles by Gudmand-Høyer and Graae were the seeds of inspiration for many Danish cohousers. In our interviews, residents repeatedly referred to one or the other of the articles as the stimulus for their first thoughts about cohousing alternatives, although some did not act on their interest until many years later.

In 1968, Bodil Graae, Jan Gudmand-Høyer, and the few families remaining from the Hareskov group joined forces with others interested in building a cohousing community. They found a building site in Jonstrup, a small village outside Copenhagen. The property is located near a military airfield, and some group members, fearing future increases in air traffic and noise, formed a second group which eventually purchased a site near the town of Hillerød. (Fortunately, there has actually been only a minimal increase in air traffic at Jonstrup.)

Through much of the planning process, the two groups worked in parallel, holding meetings in the same building and sharing information. Neither faced neighborhood opposition this time, but both were hit with new setbacks: construction bids were much higher than expected, and a loan promised to the Jonstrup group was withdrawn because of a credit squeeze. Design proposals had to be simplified to cut construction costs, causing another year's delay. Determined to realize their goal, both groups persisted, and in the end they succeeded. In the fall of 1972, 27 families moved into Saettedammen in Hillerød, designed by Teo Bjerg and Palle Dyreborg. A year later, Skraplanet's 33 families moved into the community in Jonstrup designed by Jan Gudmand-Høyer.

The 33 residences at Skraplanet are situated on the sloped site so that every living room has a view to the south. Site plan: 1. parking, 2. community plaza, 3. play ground, 4. swimming pool, 5. common house, 6. tennis court, 7. soccer field.

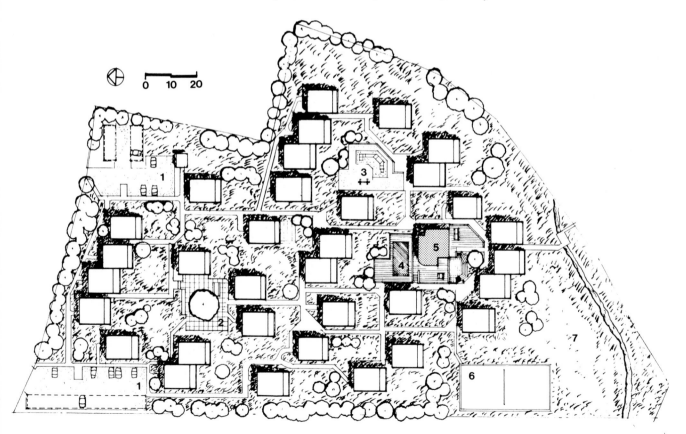

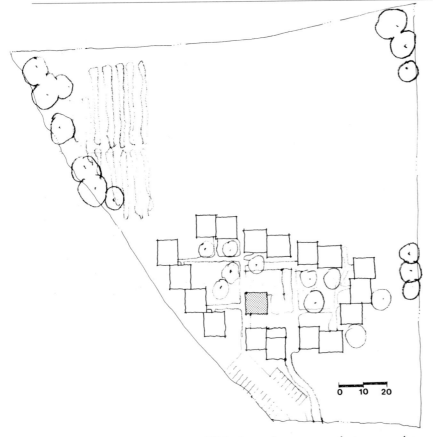

Nonbo Hede, a 15-unit community designed by Frank Vestergård, was completed in 1976.

While Saettedammen was being completed, several young families on the Danish peninsula of Jutland were discussing how they could share more of their lives than the occasional dinner or child's birthday party. This group had started to organize an effort to build a housing community before hearing of either Saettedammen or Skraplanet. Clearly, cohousing was an idea whose time had come. When the Jutland group heard of Skraplanet and Saettedammen, they consulted Gudmand-Høyer and visited both projects. For those in the middle of seemingly endless planning sessions, meetings, and battles with banks and government authorities, it was undoubtedly an inspiration to see communities built by other groups who had themselves begun with only a dream. In 1976 the Jutland group completed the third Danish cohousing community—Nonbo Hede near Viborg.

The majority of residents in these first developments were two-income families who chose cohousing as an alternative to the conventional single-family houses occupied by 65 percent of the Danish population. They were consistently attracted by the social aspects of cohousing, especially the benefits for children. It is significant that the early initiators of cohousing, though they could have afforded large, modern houses, chose smaller residences, assumed the financial risks, and spent the extra time to develop a cohousing community instead.

These early cohousing communities were practical first steps toward the ideals put forth by Gudmand-Høyer and Bodil Graae, but they were never considered the embodiment of all that cohousing should be. From the perspective of the ongoing youthful protest movement, these were nothing more than nice suburban developments for people who could afford private ownership. One Danish architecture professor called them "dentist collectives," referring to the many professionals who lived in the first cohousing communities. Although the initiators had sought a more diverse mixture of resident ages and incomes, social and financial realities called for compromise if the projects were to be built at all.

As early as 1968, Gudmand-Høyer was working with a group of teachers and parents from a small private school to develop a more collective and integrated cohousing project. Known as the Farum Project (after the town where it was to be built), the design called for dwellings for families and singles clustered around an interior common area, with the clusters connected by a glass-covered pedestrian street. The common area, including kitchen, dining room, sitting areas, and activity rooms, opened onto the covered street, and a kindergarten and the first four grades of the school were integrated with the residences.

At a housing exhibition in 1970, the Farum proposal attracted the interest of several nonprofit housing developers. The resident group pursued the possibility of working with one of these developers so as to include rental units affordable to lower-income households. Unfortunately, after several years of frustration, this joint effort was shelved due to economic and legislative complications.

Meanwhile, the Danish Building Research Institute was moving beyond technical research to examine the social implications of the physical environment. In 1971 the institute sponsored a national design competition for low-rise, clustered housing. All of the winning proposals emphasized common facilities and resident participation in the design. A new architectural firm called Vandkunsten (the firm that was later to design Trudeslund) took first place with a proposal that was essentially a manifesto calling for a cooperative society and humane communities that integrate work, housing, and recreation. The competition was well publicized, and Vandkunsten's proposal in particular had tremendous impact on the Danish housing debate. Five years later, following a participatory design process with potential residents, endless battles with bureaucrats, and many compromises, Tinggarden, a 79-unit housing development designed by Vandkunsten, was completed. Based on their prize-winning 1971 competition entry design, the project was sponsored by the institute, who subsidized the participatory process, and built by a nonprofit housing developer.

Tinggarden is divided into six clusters of 12 to 15 units surrounding a common house used for dining, meetings, and any other functions the particular cluster desires. A large meeting house serves the whole development. Although the architects and the institute attempted to maintain a democratic design process, residents ultimately did not

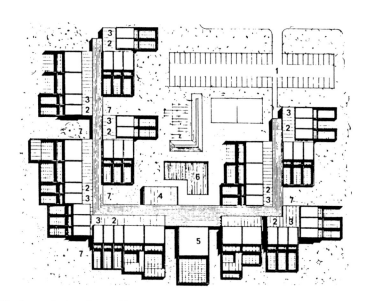

The Farum Project, designed by Jan Gudmand-Høyer in 1970, connected dwellings and common facilities along a glass-covered street. 1. parking, 2. hobby and crafts rooms, 3. semiprivate areas, 4. community rooms, 5. kindergarten, 6. swimming pool, 7. playground.

control decisions and the large majority dropped out during the long planning process. Nevertheless, Tinggarden is generally recognized as the first rental cohousing development, and as one of the best examples of government-subsidized nonprofit housing. Other Danish nonprofit housing developers have since followed suit.[4]

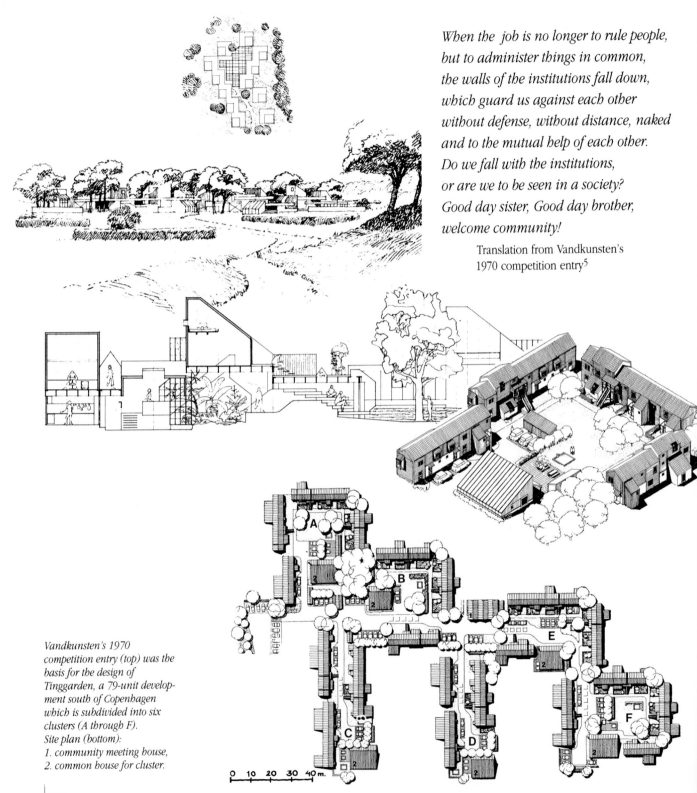

*When the job is no longer to rule people,
but to administer things in common,
the walls of the institutions fall down,
which guard us against each other
without defense, without distance, naked
and to the mutual help of each other.
Do we fall with the institutions,
or are we to be seen in a society?
Good day sister, Good day brother,
welcome community!*

Translation from Vandkunsten's
1970 competition entry[5]

*Vandkunsten's 1970 competition entry (top) was the basis for the design of Tinggarden, a 79-unit development south of Copenhagen which is subdivided into six clusters (A through F).
Site plan (bottom):
1. community meeting house,
2. common house for cluster.*

0 10 20 30 40 m.

The Concept Takes Hold

One by one, groups of people organized to realize their dream of building cohousing. Many never got past the planning stage, discouraged by roadblocks that seemed to appear at every turn. Some families were forced to drop out because construction costs proved to be more than expected and beyond their means. Nevertheless, by 1980, 12 owner-occupied cohousing communities, ranging in size from 6 to 36 households, had been built in Denmark. With one exception (Gyndbjerg), all were initiated by people who wanted to live there, and future residents participated in the planning and design process in all of them. Between 1980 and 1982, the number of cohousing communities nearly doubled, increasing from 12 to 22, with 10 others planned. The concept had taken hold.

But it still took great determination for these people to realize their goal. The development process often took as long as three to five years. Local officials and neighbors continued to have many misconceptions about cohousing, and often opposed new proposals in the belief that cohousing would hurt surrounding property values. By the late 1970s, interest rates and construction costs were undergoing unprecedented increases, creating further difficulties for cohousing organizers.

SAMBO: The Association for Cohousing.

As an advocate, consultant, and architect for several of these first cohousing projects, Jan Gudmand-Høyer was aware of the difficulties faced by new groups. To assist people through the difficult planning stages, in 1978 Gudmand-Høyer and a group of other architects, lawyers, building technicians, and social scientists formed a support association called SAMBO (roughly translated as "live together"). According to Gudmand-Høyer:

We started SAMBO because most of us were living in cohousing and believed in the idea, but also because we wanted our professional lives to assume more social relevance. Through the association, professionals with experience in this type of work and a firm belief in the concept could assist people who needed consulting and technical skills to start their own community.

The association held regular meetings and published a monthly newsletter with information on available building sites, articles on past experiences, and advertisements about newly forming groups.[6]

Several communities in the Copenhagen area were started through SAMBO, among them Jernstoberiet, Trudeslund, and Ibsgarden. Ironically, it was just such accomplishments that contributed to the association's disbanding in 1982. Once prospective groups had formed, consultants and members focused on planning their communities. Although they had planned to collaborate and share information through SAMBO, the active members' involvement in the association diminished once they had achieved their immediate aims—whether securing employment or a place to live.

New Financing Possibilities.

In 1981, the Ministry of Housing enacted new legislation making it easier and less expensive to finance cohousing. The new law was intended to boost the sagging building industry, which because of high interest rates had fallen to its lowest activity level since World War II. Fortunately, this law coincidentally provided an ideal method for financing cohousing. By providing government-sponsored, index-linked loans for new construction to any group establishing a housing cooperative of at least eight units, the law decreased the initial investment and monthly mortgage payments. To qualify for a loan, a cooperative must limit construction costs per square meter, and the average unit size must be no more than 1,023 square feet (95 square meters; m²). As members of a cooperative, residents receive the tax advantages of ownership, but their equity in the development is limited by the government, increasing according to the rate of inflation rather than speculative market rates. [7]

The Cooperative Housing Association Law was a windfall for cohousing. Ebbe Klovedal and Poul Bjere wrote in 1984:

In these provisions hides a previously unknown possibility for people who have wanted to establish a cohousing community but who haven't had the money to do it. . . . If utilized appropriately, cohousing will now be for many people the cheapest way to establish a home.

Besides making cohousing more affordable, the loan requirements force cohousing groups to clarify their priorities and encourage them to seek greater diversity in household composition—a long-standing goal. As a result of this law, many cohousing groups have decided to limit the average unit size to ten percent below the allowed maximum (1,023 square feet), so as to allocate more area to common facilities. In order to build some units larger than the average for families with several children, groups must make an extra effort to find single- and two-person households for smaller units.

Since 1981, most Danish cohousing communities have been structured as limited-equity cooperatives financed with government-sponsored loans. Nonprofit housing associations also have built more rental cohousing developments that permit rent subsidies for qualifying low-income residents. By early 1988, four complete communities and half of another, totaling 277 units, were functioning successfully as nonprofit-owned rentals, and another six cohousing projects were being built by nonprofit developers.

Increasing Diversity Among Residents. Expanded financing possibilities have produced a more diversified cohousing resident mix. Whereas earlier communities consisted almost exclusively of two-income families with children, a sampling of six cooperatively financed communities built between 1983 and 1985 shows the households to be 16 percent single persons, 29 percent single parents, 1 percent couples without children, and 54 percent couples with children. The diversity is even greater in a sample of three nonprofit-owned rentals built between 1978 and 1982—28 percent singles, 36 percent single parents, 14 percent couples without children, and 22 percent couples with children.

Adult residents range in age from early 20s to mid-70s. The majority move into cohousing between the ages of 30 and 45, but the number of elderly participants is increasing steadily. Several communities have been initiated by seniors as an alternative to housing for the elderly. Today, cohousing is cross-generational, attracting singles, single parents, couples without children, families, and seniors.

Although all types of occupations are represented among residents, teaching and public-sector jobs are the most common. Most have a college education, and even though resident diversity is increasing, cohousing is still largely a white-collar, middle-class phenomenon. It is difficult to say exactly why more people in blue-collar occupations are not represented in cohousing communities. Perhaps the values associated with the concept, such as nonhierarchical decision making and nongender-based roles, tend to be white-collar concerns in Denmark. (Wages for skilled workers are relatively high in Denmark, so affordability is not the issue.) Hans S. Andersen, an engineer with the Danish Building Research Institute and a cohousing resident, writes in an article for *Scandinavian Housing and Planning Research*: "In fact, the importance of practical activities favors people with practical skills, and craftsmen are highly esteemed in the [cohousing] cooperatives that have them. The main problem is that it requires intellectual skills and talents for organization to *establish* the cooperative." As cohousing continues to gain greater acceptance by the general public, it attracts a broader representation of occupations.

The most important factor in determining who lives in cohousing is not income, but rather a personal commitment to getting a project built. Low turnover rates (averaging 3.3 percent a year) and long waiting lists for available units often force people who want to live in cohousing to start their own development. In fact, many communities have been initiated by people on waiting lists for others, so that two or three developments may end up being built near each other.

Current Trends

Cohousing is now a well-established housing option in Denmark. The number of communities continues to increase at an impressive rate; in 1988 alone, at least 38 cohousing developments were in various stages of planning and/or construction. When built, these developments will result in more than a 50 percent increase in the total number of communities. In 1985, Jan Gudmand-Høyer and Angels Colom won an architectural competition for a large new housing development to be built in several stages in Ballerup, a suburb of Copenhagen. By the spring of 1988, they were designing eleven cohousing communities of 20 to 40 dwellings (300 units in all) as the first phase

of 48 resident-managed cohousing communities to be built in the next several years in Ballerup. Of these eleven (six on one site and five on another), six are nonprofit-owned rentals, three are cooperatively financed, and three are privately financed. Three of the communities are designed around cover-streets. Gudmand-Høyer wrote that:

> Our drawing studio is in the middle of the construction site so we can have optimal contact with the residents and have an ongoing exhibit of the design revisions. We hold three to four resident meetings a day. This will be the first city in the world where Thomas More's idea of Utopia is realized, some five hundred years after it was conceived.

There is a certain irony in realizing that one of these cohousing neighborhoods is being built within a mile of the original Hareskov site, where the first cohousing community was planned and defeated. Hans S. Andersen told us:

Henning Kristensen, a retiree and cohousing resident, told us: "It's exceptional here. . . . It's wonderful to live with people of so many different ages and backgrounds. We all do different things. Some people are good at carpentry; I prune the trees, and others do other things.

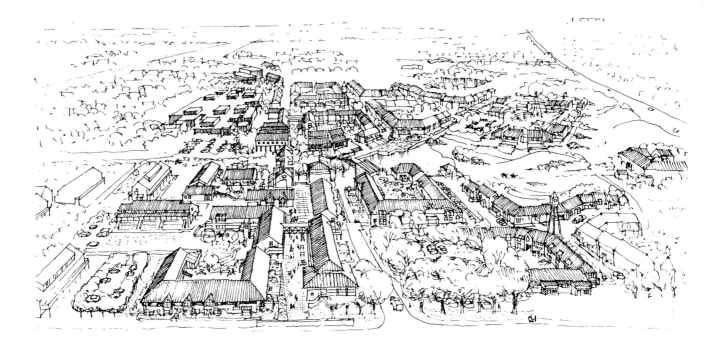

New housing area outside of Copenhagen (Egebjerggard, Ballerup) in which 48 cohousing communities will be built in four phases.

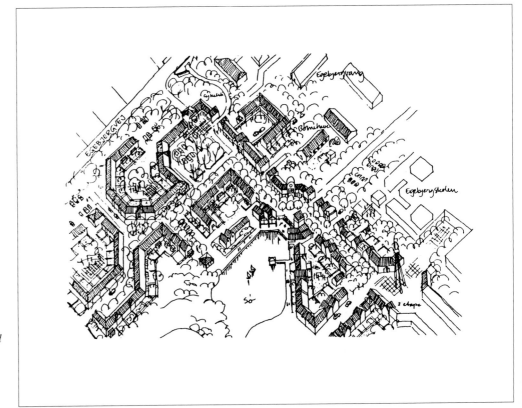

The first phase of the Egebjerggard development includes one privately financed community, three cooperatives, and one nonprofit-owned rental complex, designed by Jan Gudmand-Høyer and Angels Colom.

It makes sense that the popularity of cohousing has grown so. As more people move into cohousing communities, more people—friends, neighbors, and relatives—find out what this way of living is all about and see its advantages. Then they want to try it themselves.

The reaction of one resident's parents is characteristic:

When we announced our plans to sell our house and move into a cohousing community, my parents thought we were crazy. My mother assumed it would be only temporary and that in a short time we would miss our old house. But once they came to visit, attended a common dinner, and talked to the other people here, they began to understand why we wanted to live like this. Now they're talking with their friends about building a cohousing community.

The concept of cohousing has continually evolved since Jan Gudmand-Høyer began discussing his ideas for a cooperative living environment more than two decades ago. The average size of individual residences in new communities is almost half of what it was at Saettedammen and Skraplanet. While individual residences have decreased in size, shared facilities have increased in relative proportion and importance. The range of

unit sizes and the mixture of residents and household types has greatly diversified. Previous criticisms of cohousing as a high-priced option out of reach of common people no longer hold true.

The buildings themselves reflect this evolutionary process. Cohousing residents have chosen to cluster their dwellings closer and closer together, as is especially evident in the new communities that connect ground-level dwellings and common facilities under one roof. Gudmand-Høyer first proposed this design in response to the northern climate and its drastic effect on the use of outdoor areas in his 1970 Farum Project, which was never built. In 1981, the Jernstoberiet community reused the central hall of an iron foundry as a covered courtyard between individual residences and common facilities—for the first time actually incorporating this concept in cohousing. By 1988, seven more communities had incorporated glass-covered streets or courts, indicating a continuing trend in this direction.

The increasing willingness of residents to live close together reflects growing confidence in the cohousing concept, as people recognize its benefits and learn from existing communities. The Danish cohousing communities being built today would not be designed as they are had not the earlier, more conservative developments preceded them. Greater proximity of dwellings is only possible when cohousing maintains the deli-

With 32 dwellings lining a glass-covered street, Handvaerkerparken, designed by Arkitektgruppenin Aarhus, is one of a growing number of cohousing developments that connect residences and common facilities with glass-covered walkways.

145

With new technologies, more people work at home, but few take their afternoon break at a community tea time like this resident of Trudeslund.

cate balance between privacy and community and protects residents' ability to choose between the two.

After initial skepticism, cohousing has won the support of the Danish government and financial institutions. The Danish Building Research Institute and the Building Development Council have both recognized cohousing as one of the few residential models to address the demographic and economic changes in Western industrial societies. Both organizations have published reports on the experiences of cohousing communities, including one which looks to cohousing as a model for the future as technology allows more people to work in the home.[8] They also have given financial support to several communities for specific design innovations, and the Development Council sponsored a two-day conference on cohousing in 1985. At that conference, architect Philip Arctander summed up in his closing statement:

> *A community can in many situations give better help than an institution; but the larger community, society, must supply the safety net. With this reservation, the seminar found great possibilities in the further development of the cohousing*

idea. . . . Cohousing has the possibility to be a part of a new way of handling society's problems. Not privatizing, not institutionalizing, but collectivizing.

Banks were once reluctant to loan to cohousing groups, but today such developments are generally "preferred risk." Banks are particularly attracted because most cohousing units are pre-sold long before construction is completed—a record with which few other housing developments can compete. Cohousing developments also have an excellent track record of good management.

Recently, some of the basic ideas of cohousing have been adopted by developers of speculative and subsidized housing who have recognized that this model addresses the needs of a growing segment of the population. In 1982, residents of a modern 1,500-unit nonprofit housing project, Farum Midpunkt, converted a section to cohousing in order to overcome problems of vandalism and high resident turnover. Residents in the 57-unit cohousing block organized community activities such as a dining club, Friday night pub, Saturday cafe, and seasonal festivities. They not only created better conditions in their own housing block, but their efforts encouraged other residents to make changes in the rest of the development. In 1985, the complex was fully occupied for the first time in five years.

In a 1984 national design competition for a large (several-hundred-unit) publicly assisted housing development, all of the winning entries divided the project into clusters of 20 to 40 units sharing a common house. Common facilities included much more than the conventional laundry room—kitchens and dining areas for dinner clubs and parties, meeting rooms, and children's play areas. These designs recognize the advantages of breaking large developments into smaller groups to encourage a stronger sense of communal responsibility, resulting in lower maintenance costs and less resident turnover.

Speculative housing developers have also found cohousing design concepts to be very marketable. Condominium developments, which for decades have been designed for maximum individual privacy, are increasingly incorporating site planning concepts that encourage casual interaction among residents. One example is the high-priced development Sjolund, where parking at the edge of the site leaves the rest of the development open for pedestrians, and individual terraces face the walkways and children's play areas. In an article about this development, the project architects explain: "People want some sort of community, or they wouldn't pay so much money to live so closely together."

Even in older neighborhoods of single-family houses, groups have organized dinner clubs where three or four families eat together once a week, rotating among houses. It is impossible to say whether these ideas were taken directly from cohousing, were learned from friends or the media, or are simply responses to social and economic realities. Nevertheless, it is obvious that as people see the advantages of a more practical and social living environment, they assign higher priority to design and planning that encourages these qualities.

The Future of Cohousing

As the first generation of children raised in cohousing comes of age and moves out on their own, it is clear that this approach to housing is more than a passing fad. The teenage residents of the first cohousing communities generally want to experience other housing environments, such as student dorms, shared houses, and inner-city apartments, but most of them expect to live in

cohousing again. "I can't imagine raising children any other way," one teenager told us. Better than anyone, they know the benefits of growing up in cohousing. As they and future generations mature, the cohousing concept will continue to evolve, adjusting to their changing needs and interests.

The trend toward working part or full time at home is already apparent. Having a greater number of residents at home during the day can further enrich community life and eliminate the social isolation that often results from working alone at home. The computer "network" at Trudeslund, installed as part of a government study, explores this option. Another possibility being discussed by cohousers is the provision of office space in the common house, where several people could share resources such as a copy machine, computer, and secretarial support. In his book *The Third Wave*, Alvin Toffler argues that such neighborhood work centers and the "electronic cottage" will become more and more attractive as commuting becomes more difficult.

There is also a growing trend toward building new communities next to existing cohousing developments—as in Birkerod, where Trudeslund, Tornevangsgarden, and Andedammen are located, and two other communities are planned. In Beder, residents from a 21-unit townhouse development (Midgarden), situated between the cohousing communities of Sun and Wind and Vildrosen, decided to build a common house themselves after observing firsthand its usefulness. Gudmand-Høyer's latest projects in Ballerup illustrate how large new housing developments can be broken into smaller cohousing clusters. Pooling the resources and people of several communities makes possible activities that can be difficult for one community to support, such as child care and senior programs, dance and theater classes, and other cultural events. Whereas neighbors in traditional communities must be contacted household by household, in cohousing developments residents can communicate quickly by simply tacking a notice on the community bulletin board. As cohousing becomes more commonplace and the barriers of suspicion break down, we are also likely to see more integration between communities and their surrounding neighbors.

Cohousing in Other Countries

While cohousing was pioneered in Denmark and the largest number of cohousing developments are located there, other European countries—most notably the Netherlands—are now exploring similar concepts. Developed with little knowledge of their Danish counterparts, the Dutch *centraal wonen* ("central living") incorporate the same characteristics as Danish cohousing—common facilities, resident initiated and planned, intentional neighborhood design, and complete resident management—but they differ in the placement of common facilities. In Denmark, most common facilities are centrally located for use by the whole development; in the Netherlands, clusters of four to eight households usually share a living, kitchen, and dining area. As a result, the common facilities for the entire development are generally smaller and do not include dining areas. While this allows the clusters a more intimate shared space, it reduces the advantages of cooperating on a larger scale for meals. It takes greater individual effort for the small clusters to organize regular dining and other functions, which sometimes detracts from involvement with the larger community. One resident commented, "People can become so involved with their cluster that they forget about the larger group, while other clusters don't have the energy to organize any activities."

The first cohousing project built in the Netherlands was the 50-unit Hilversum community, designed by Leo de Longe and Pieter Weeda. When it was completed in 1977 after six years of planning, the residents received so many requests for information that they organized a national organization of *centraal wonen* to help new groups. Ten years after Hilversum was completed, 30 other cohousing communities had been built in the Netherlands, and approximately 40 are planned.

In Sweden there has been renewed interest in the *kollektivhus*, or "housing with services," a model first developed in the 1930s. The *kollektivhus* differs from Danish cohousing in that it is usually instigated and developed by housing professionals or local authorities, resulting in more institutional approaches. Most of the Swedish examples are high-rise buildings, and over half contain more than 50 units (up to 186 units). In some cases, residents are not involved in management of the complex and pay for communal services such as dining.[9]

The Swedes have been very successful in rehabilitating problem-ridden, high-rise complexes built in the 1960s and '70s by adding common facilities and involving residents in management. One of these is Stacken, a 33-unit, nine-story high-rise located outside of Goteborg which was more than 60 percent vacant just ten years after it was built. In 1980, it was converted to cohousing with the addition of a common dining room, a child-care program, workshops, and laundry facilities. Although the common facilities have greatly improved Stacken's livability, residents still express frustration with living in a high-rise building. The Danes have built similar housing with services, but have done little with this model since the 1950s.

Cohousing projects have also been built in Norway, Germany, and France. One Norwegian architect we met commented, "We like to let the Danes do the experimenting.

In the 50-unit Hilversum development, designed by Leo de Longe and Pieter Weeda, clusters of five dwellings share a common kitchen, dining, and living room; a, (each dwelling also has its own kitchenette). Additional facilities, b, are shared by the whole development.

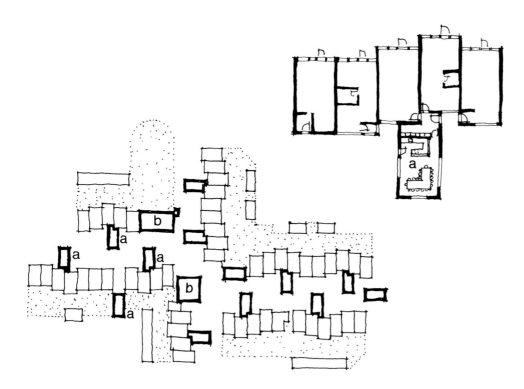

When it is clear that an idea works, then we try it."

With all Western industrialized nations facing similar changes in demographics and lifestyles, improved communications between countries would greatly benefit people trying to find responsive housing alternatives. Two decades ago, Danish cohousing initiators faced many of the same barriers to new housing ideas that we face in the United States today. By building on their experience and learning from their mistakes, perhaps we can avoid some common problems (although there will undoubtedly be new ones) and make the development of cohousing less difficult both in the United States and in other countries.

Notes

1. Jan Gudmand-Høyer, "Ikke kun huse for folk—ogsa huse af folk," *Information* (April 4, 1984).

2. Ibid.,

3. Ibid.,

4. Published in *Taet-lav—en boligform Idekonkurrence* (Statens Byggeforskningsinstitut, Rapport 82, 1972), 31.

5. Danish nonprofit housing is generally built and administered by local nonprofit housing associations in which the tenants are represented on the executive committees, or make them up completely. No private capital interests or profits are accepted in these associations and dwelling sizes and construction costs are subject to central and local government control. Rent is calculated as a purely economic cost-price rent; that is, rent is calculated to balance operational costs, interest, and amortization. Nonprofit housing is financed with index-linked loans of up to 80 percent (75 percent before 1984) from private mortgage credit institutions with government payment of interest. Central and local governments provide favorable loans for most of the remaining portion (18–23 percent) of construction costs and guarantee part of the mortgage credit financing. These low-interest or interest-free loans are used along with direct construction grants and individual subsidies for low-income households to make nonprofit rentals more affordable than market rate housing. The nonprofit sector has built up to 50 percent of all new dwellings in Denmark in recent years. For more information see *Financing of Housing in Denmark* (Ministry of Housing, Copenhagen, 1984).

6. A Danish employment program, which paid 85 percent of the consultants' fees, provided financial support.

7. This cooperative structure is similar in concept to limited-equity cooperatives in the United States, whose resale values are also limited by the government according to the rate of inflation.

8. *Boliger og Boformer i Informations-samfundet* (Housing and Living Forms in the Information Society), BUR, 1984.

9. Hans S. Andersen, "Danish Low-rise Housing Cooperatives as an Example of a Local Community Organization," *Scandinavian Housing and Planning Research* (May 1985): 63. A description of communal housing in Sweden can be found in a paper by Alison Woodward in *Housing for Nontraditional Households*, a forthcoming book edited by Karen Franck and Sherie Ahrentzen (Van Nostrand Reinhold).

DANISH COHOUSING AND COMMON FACILITIES [1]

#	COMMUNITY	YEAR BUILT	# OF UNITS	TENURE [2]	SIZE OF COMMON HOUSE (s.f.)	COMMON AREA PER UNIT (s.f.)	MEALS/WEEK [3]	LIVING ROOM	LAUNDRY	CHILDREN'S RMS [5]	CHILD CARE [4]	TEEN/MUSIC RMS	WORKSHOP(S) [5]	STORE OR FOOD CLUB	GUEST/RENTAL ROOM	SITE PLAN (E)=Existing CH=Common House
1	Sættedammen	1972	27	Private (P)	3,010	112	6d	X	X	X	X	2		X	2	2 Courtyards
2	Skråplanet	1973	33	P	3,770	114	5d	X	X	X	X	1				Semi-detached terraced houses
3	Nonbo Hede	1974-76	15	P	3,530	235	3	X	X	X		2			4	2 Clusters
4	Gyldenmuld	1976	12	P	3,900	325	5	X	X						2	Cluster
5	Gyndbjerg	"	14	P	2,150	154	4	X	X		X	1	X	X		Street/CH in (E) farm house
6	Drejerbanken	1978	20	P & Rental	5,110	226	7	X	X	X	X	2				2 Courtyards
7	Tinggården	"	79	Rental	9,680	122	0-2	X	X	X	X	4			16	6 clusters w/separate CH's
8	Tornevangsgård	"	6	P	2,040	340	2	X	X	X	X	1			1	Courtyard /CH in (E) bldg.
9	Jerngården	"	8	P	2,010	251	7	X	X	X		2				Renovated rowhouses
10	Æblevangen	1979	36	P	6,460	179	6	X	X	X	X	3				4 courtyards
11	Mejdal 1	"	12	P	2,150	179	3	X	X	X		1				Clustered detached single family houses
12	Stavnsbåndet	"	26	P	5,170	199	4+	X	X	X	X			X	1	Street / 3 rentals in (E) bldg.
13	Bakken	1980	25	P	5,800	232	5	X	X	X		2			3	Reused school bldg.
14	Bofælleden	"	8	Private Coop.	?	?	7	X	X	X		1	X			Detached single family houses
15	Faldengrund	"	12	P	3,860	322	5	X	X	X	X	2	X	X	3	4 clusters
16	Frugthaven	"	12	P	2,480	207	4	X	X	X	X	1			1	Rowhouses
17	Gug	"	22	P	4,520	205	7	X	X	X	X	2			6	Rowhouses
18	Overdrevet	"	25	P	6,840	274	7	X	X	X	X	2	X	X	1	2 courtyards
19	Sol & Vind	"	27	P	5,920	219	7	X	X	X	X	2	X	X	2	Streets & courts/50% detached houses
20	Vildrosen	"	12	P	4,306	359	5	X	X	X	X	3	X	X	1	3 courtyards /detached houses
21	Jernstøberiet	1981	21	P	3,230	154	5	X	X	X		1	X	X		Reuse of factory bldg. /interior court
22	Kolbotten	"	6	P	1,185	197	5	X	X	X	X	1				Units & CH attached
23	Trudeslund	"	33	P	8,610	261	7	X	X	X	X	2	X	X	1	Street
24	Bondebjerget	1982-83	80	Rental	15,500	194	3-7	X	X	X		8	X	X		4 clusters w/separate CH's
25	Drivhuset	1983	18	Cooperative	2,530	140	5	X	X	X	X	2	X	X	4	Glass covered street
26	Grønnegård	"	7	P	3,230	461	4	X	X	X	X	1			1	Rowhouses w/ CH in (E) farm house
27	Ibsgården	"	21	Cooperative	3,730	178	7	X	X	X	X	1	X	X		Courtyard w/ CH in (E) farm house
28	Nørgårds Plantage	"	24	Cooperative	1,185	49	2	X	X	X		1				Streets w/carport next to each home
29	Uldalen	"	18	Cooperative	2,700	150	5	X	X	X		1			3	Reuse of factory bldgs. + new rowhouses
30	Vejgård Bymidte	"	40	P	1,350	34	5	X								Courtyard
31	Abakken	1984	15	Cooperative	4,430	295	3	X	X	X	X	1			5	Rowhouses w/ CH in (E) bldg.
32	Andedammen	"	18	Cooperative	3,000	167	7	X	X	X	X	1	X			Rowhouses
33	Askebakken	"	17	Cooperative	2,820	166	5	X	X	X		2			2	Glass covered street
34	Savværket	"	21	Cooperative	4,310	205	7	X	X	X	X	3	X	X	4	Glass covered street
35	Blåhøjen	1985	25	Cooperative	5,920	237	7	X	X	X		1	X	X	1	3 Courtyards
36	Håndværkerparken	"	32	Rental	5,670	177	5	X	X	X	X	2			2	Glass covered street
37	Mejdal II	"	14	P	1,600	114	?	X	X	X						Clustered detached single family houses
38	Thorshammar I	1986	20	Cooperative	3,230	162	7	X	X	X		3			4	Courtyard w/glass covered walkway

X Includes at least one such facility.

1 Subset of total of 46 cohousing communities studied by the authors in 1984/85. All have common kitchens and dining rooms, and many have additional facilities not shown here. Covered street space and out buildings are not included in size.

2 Private refers to forms of ownership similar to condominums. Cooperatives use government-sponsored financing which limits members' equity. Rentals are owned by private, non-profit housing developers.

3 "d" represents weekly dinner clubs in which residents typically participate once or twice a week, although dinners are available five to six times a week.

4 Child care is readily available in Denmark and therefore not a high priority in cohousing. Danish communities often organize programs when they have a group of similar age kids and switch to other facilities when there is less need. Both past and current programs have been included.

5 Includes wood working, bicycle repair, auto repair, photographic dark rooms, sewing, and craft work spaces.

CHAPTER THIRTEEN

For every ten families who want to live in cohousing, there is only one that is prepared to take on the burden of the planning period, and for every ten of those, there are only a few who can take the initiative.

Jan Gudmand-Høyer[1]

From Dream to Reality:
The Development Process

R esident participation in the development process is cohousing's greatest asset and its most limiting factor. It is a huge task for a group of people, inexperienced in both collective decision making and the building industry, to take on a project of this complexity. Most residents have little knowledge of financing, design, and construction issues for housing development. They encounter problems in maintaining an efficient timeline, avoiding the domination of a few strong personalities, and integrating new members without backtracking. Luckily, in dealing with these issues today, we can benefit from two decades of cohousing experience.

The participatory process has played an integral part in the evolution of cohousing. When people first discussed the concept in the mid-1960s they knew what they were rejecting—the isolation of single-family houses and apartments—but not what they were seeking. Through group discussions they pieced together a realistic alternative. Later groups built on these ideas, each reevaluating priorities and the degree of community desired. Through these discussions, and the lessons learned from previous experiences, cohousing evolved.

As cohousing becomes better known and more clearly defined, the participatory process itself evolves. When a new *bofællesskab* is advertised in Denmark today, people know what it is. Groups begin the planning process by visiting existing cohousing developments. Features now taken for granted, such as common dining and smaller individual residences, required months of discussion in earlier projects. The first cohousing projects took from five to eight years to develop; today it can take as little as two years from the first meetings to moving in.

This chapter gives an overview of the participatory development process, with an eye toward the lessons we can learn from past experience. Issues that are regionally specific, such as site identification, acquisition methods, and financing options, are not discussed in detail because the Danish experience is of little help in other countries.

Overview of the Development Process

The development process for every cohousing community is different. In some cases, the group forms with the intention of developing a specific site. In others, the group establishes its goals and objectives before identifying a site. Often, program development and site acquisition are carried out simultaneously. The cohousing development process generally includes the following phases, although the sequence may vary:

Getting Started
- find others interested in proposal
- establish an organizing group
- agree on general goals, location, and financial expectations

Preparing a Development Program
- define organizational structure and decision-making procedures; draw up initial legal agreement
- specify goals and establish priorities
- choose consultants—architect, financial consultant, attorney, etc.
- identify potential sites
- formulate development strategy: consider financing options, concerns of officials, residents' role, project timeline
- consider design objectives and requirements
- draw up legal agreements for partnership or joint venture arrangement
- acquire site
- Complete the development program

Design and Construction Documents
- develop schematic design proposal
- design development
- obtain planning approvals
- clarify financing arrangements
- complete working drawings and building specifications
- obtain building permits
- solicit and negotiate construction bids
- select contractor
- finalize construction contract, loan, and schedule

Construction
- monitor contracted work
- complete resident-built work

Move in!

Getting Started

The development process often begins when the initiating households place a notice about the proposed project in a local newspaper to attract other participants. Several groups have experienced the frustration of attracting too many people before setting the basic parameters of the project. The Sun and Wind group, for instance, attracted over one hundred people to their first meeting and then spent a year and a half discussing their goals. With new people continually coming into the group, previously resolved issues often resurfaced and had to be discussed again. When a site was finally chosen, half the group dropped out anyway.

For a more timely development process, groups have found it easier to start with an organizing, or core, group of five to fifteen households, who define general goals, identify a site, and establish financial expectations. Once these decisions have been made, other people can decide if they are interested in the project. Indeed, as a project becomes more clearly defined, more people are attracted to it. Lars Bjerre, who initiated the community he now lives in and consulted on several others, commented:

> You need at least one burning soul who really wants to live there to carry a project through. If you have one to four burning souls, then there is no problem. Others will become interested when it begins to smell like something real.

The Danish Building Development Council advises in their report *Way to Cohousing*:

> The first and most important question is: which characteristics and what extent of community does the group want?

This can be a difficult question for the group to answer initially because few people have a clear opinion. How do you know how often you will want to eat in the common house if you have never experienced common meals? Discussing individual expectations helps to clarify the group's primary goals and objectives, the common activities desired, and the financial capabilities.

A second closely related issue is the desired size of the community and resident composition. The number of households will ultimately be determined by the size of the site. If a site has not yet been identified, the initiators should agree on the general size of the community they seek.

Size. The size of the community influences resident composition as well as the type of common facilities. For instance, 12 households will not be capable of supporting child-care facilities unless a majority of the households have children near the same age. "What is the best size?" is one of the questions we are most frequently asked. While theorists have put forward many hypotheses over the centuries, we have drawn our conclusions directly from the opinions expressed by hundreds of cohousing residents, and from our own observations. To put it quite simply, it depends—on personal preferences, location, and the organizing group's goals.

The size of cohousing developments is generally discussed in terms of number of households, but the size of those households must also be considered. In a 20-unit development where 80 percent of the households consist of two adults, there are 12 more people to share the preparation of common dinners than in a 20-unit development where 80 percent of the households consist of only one adult. In the following discussion we have assumed that at least half of the households have two adults.

Our research indicates that residents categorize communities in three general sizes: small (6 to 12 households), medium (15 to 30 households), and large (35 plus). These categories are obviously not precise, and communities between these sizes have attributes of the categories on either side. The differences actually vary along a continuum.

In small cohousing developments (6 to 12 households) the residents know each other well; it's more like an extended family. Medium-sized cohousing (15 to 30 households) seems to be optimal. When asked what they thought the best size would be, the great majority of cohousers answered somewhere between 18 and 25, regardless of which size the respondents lived in. Large cohousing (35-80 households) tends to be more institutional, both in feeling and operation.

The lower size limits are dictated largely by practical considerations. Although there are some communities with less than six dwellings, it is hard to justify the cost of

common facilities and the effort to coordinate activities for so few households. With four households, for example, if half of the residents participate in the common dinner on any given night, the two households that attend hardly make the coordination and effort worthwhile. With less than six households it is can be difficult to organize consistent and reliable common activities, and reliability is essential if common activities are to work. In a community of this size, everyone must be good friends, an aspect which limits the community's long-term possibilities.

Small Cohousing Developments (6 to 12 households). Small cohousing developments are simpler to organize and require less land, making it easier to find good sites. Small projects are also less likely to attract neighborhood opposition, and are more comprehensible to planning and financing institutions. Managing a small cohousing development is less complicated and less formal, because fewer people are involved; most adults participate in what is as much a discussion as a meeting.

Some small communities initially intended to be larger but settled for fewer households when they found a smaller but attractive land parcel. "We sought a site large enough for 20 to 30 houses," explained a resident of Tornevangsgarden, "but then bought one only large enough for six dwellings because it was a great location. Although I still think six households is too small, we enjoy this place very much and wouldn't trade it now."

When we asked about the issue of size, residents of cohousing developments with 12 or fewer households often commented, "It could be a little larger." "At only six households (or eight or ten) you have to work at it," was a common sentiment. One resident explained, "It can sometimes be a little like a second marriage. You have to get along with the others; you tend to be very conscious of their feelings. If someone is missing from a common work day you notice it." On the other hand, one woman who lived in a community of 12 households told us she "simply could not imagine living in a larger community."

A small community requires more compatibility, allows less diversity, and requires a greater community commitment from each individual. If there is a serious disagreement between residents, it is more common for a household to move out, whereas in larger communities they can just avoid each other for a while. In addition, the common facilities usually require a larger financial investment per household.

Large Cohousing Developments (35 plus). A large community allows for greater diversity of ages and family types, and common facilities can be more extensive and affordable through economy of scale. The participation of a nonprofit organization is more likely with large communities, allowing for government subsidies. But planning approvals and financing arrangements are also more complex for large projects, which are also more likely to attract neighborhood opposition, further slowing the approval process. In fact, we generally do not recommend that a resident organizing group attempt to build a community of this size without collaborating with an experienced developer.

When we asked residents of large communities (even those with over 30 dwellings) about the size, nearly everyone answered, "It isn't possible to know each other as well as you'd like—it would be better if it were a little smaller."

All of the cohousing developments we know in Denmark and the Netherlands larger than 40 dwellings have been divided into smaller clusters. In Tinggarden (79 units), clusters of 12 to 15 households share a common house with only a meeting hall shared

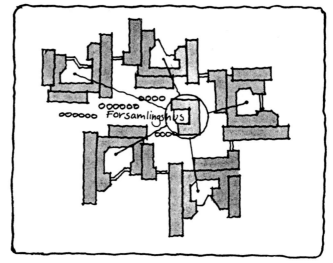

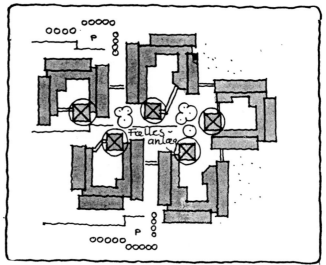

by the whole development. At Hilversum in the Netherlands (50 units), five households share a common kitchen/dining/living area so that there is no common dining in the central facilities for the whole development. The largest cohousing development in Denmark, Bondebjerget (80 units), is divided into four groups with four completely separate common houses. Even Aeblevangen, with only 36 units, built two separate common dining rooms and kitchens because the residents decided that one dining room would be so large that residents would feel

Larger developments can be subdivided into smaller clusters to retain a more intimate community atmosphere.

157

uncomfortable and participate less often.

Breaking large developments into more intimately scaled groups preserves the close sense of community that would otherwise be lost with an increase in size. Each cluster takes on its own character, and different clusters may have varying amounts of community activities. There appears to be a natural limit to the number of people who can know each other by name and share common facilities as an extension of their own home. With larger numbers of people, the group identity is diluted and personal accountability diminishes.

If large communities are not broken into smaller clusters, intimacy, cooperative workability, and even the distinction between "common" and "general public" begin to grey. Management becomes institutionalized out of sheer necessity, and people feel that they really have to assert themselves to be heard in the common meetings. Participation tends to dwindle, and management decisions are delegated to a committee. For anyone who plans to build a community of more than 40 units, we strongly recommend that the development be broken into smaller clusters.

Medium-sized Cohousing (15 to 30 households). When asked about size, residents of medium-sized cohousing developments usually thought their own was just about right. "Thirty-three houses is just right," announced Alice from behind the stove in the common house, "because you only have to cook once a month." There are 61 adults in her community, and with two cooking each night, each adult cooks just once a month. "It's small enough to know everyone, but large enough to avoid those that you don't particularly care for," was a common statement about mid-sized cohousing.

To make a case for the medium size is to make a case for cohousing itself—large

enough to have extensive shared facilities, but small enough to be managed by direct democracy. This size can more easily accommodate variations in individual schedules; it's not a big deal if several people miss a meeting or work day, but when you are there, you have direct input. While decisions are still made through the consensus-seeking process, their implementation can be distributed among the entire community. Though decision making becomes more formalized than in small communities, it can still include everyone.

If a site is not identified at the outset, it is also important for the organizing group to agree on the geographic area where they want to live, as well as the amount of open space desired. Many groups who had agreed on other objectives ended up splitting over site location, often a choice between a more urban or rural context.

Location also influences what is an appropriate size. Most of the small communities were too claustrophobic for our taste, however, we felt very comfortable at Jerngarden, which is only eight households, but is located in the center of the city. Like Goldilocks, everyone should consider the characteristics of each size to find the one that best fits their preferences and situation.

Preparing a Development Program

A cohesive development program defining the group's goals, priorities, financing capability, and design requirements establishes a strong foundation so that new members can be easily integrated, the design and construction phases made less time consuming, and costs kept down. This phase, sometimes referred to as "programming," has a broader scope in the cohousing development process than in conventional development. The development program should specify the environmental, financial, and social goals and objectives of the community. For instance, it should define the intended functions and cost limitations of the common house, rather than just its square footage.

The preparation of the program should be considered a learning period for all participants, including the architect and consultants.[2] Residents will need some understanding of the design and development process to enable them to participate in discussions and decisions. Consultants will need to understand residents' expectations. If this stage is rushed or the development program is incomplete, the project is more likely to disintegrate before it is completed.

The organizing group needs to clarify mutual expectations for the community, especially financial commitments, and to build a sense of trust among participants so that they feel confident about investing in the project together. Only then is the group capable of purchasing a site. Issues not actually included in the written development program, such as organizational structure and decision making procedures, development strategies, financing options, and legal agreements, also need to be addressed at this stage. Ideally, these issues and the development program will have been thoroughly considered before a site is acquired. Then the group can quickly finish the program (which is not complete until there is a site) and proceed with architectural design in a cost-effective manner. With rising land and financing costs, it can prove expensive and unpleasant if the group gets bogged down with these issues while paying interest on a site. The completed development program is a written document which establishes the basis for the architectural design.

Organization and Decision Making. A

participatory process need not entail endless meetings and discussions. As with any other effective business venture, efficient organizational structures and work methods must be

Issues Addressed in a Cohousing Development Program
Social Characteristics
- resident composition (diversity of household types, ages, incomes)
- children's needs
- expectations for community life and social contact
- balance between private and community life; degree of participation
- relationship to surrounding neighborhood

General Design Criteria
- number of units
- site amenities to preserve (views, trees, etc.)
- location of common facilities, residential buildings, open space
- building type and form (e.g., two stories, clusters, detached, etc.)
- building materials (general)
- energy considerations (electric, gas, solar, wind, conservation)
- handicap accessibility

Common Facilities
- functions to be accommodated (e.g., dining, children's rooms, etc.)
- priority of functions
- desired characteristics (e.g., warm, comfortable, easy to maintain, etc.)
- acoustic and light considerations; solar access visual access to private houses, site, etc.
- indoor/outdoor relationship (e.g., access to terraces, etc.)
- considerations of future needs

Individual Residences
- distribution of house types (number of studios, one-bedroom units, shared households, etc.)
- functions to be accommodated (e.g., dining, sleeping, work, etc.)
- desired characteristics (e.g., combined kitchen/dining/living room, separation between children's and adults' bedrooms, etc.)
- acoustic and light considerations
- indoor/outdoor relationship (e.g., access to terrace, etc.)
- flexibility and future additions

Outdoor Areas
- parking (e.g., location, how much, covered)
- car access on site (e.g., traffic free, access to houses when necessary)
- open space
- shared amenities (e.g., play structures, sitting areas, gardens, etc.)
- transition between private residences and common areas
- private outdoor functions (e.g., sitting, gardens, etc.)
- fences, hedges, plantings

Construction
- phases
- resident-built options

Financial Expectations
- projected unit cost (including common areas)
- projected construction cost per square foot

Projected Development Timeline

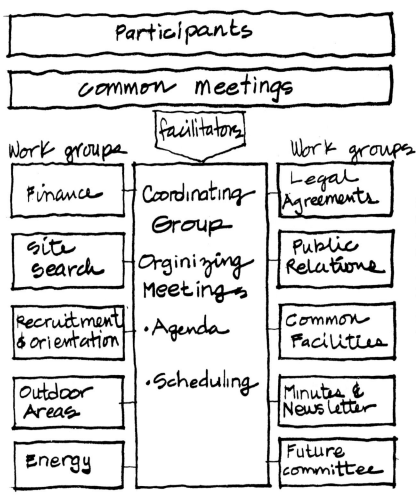

Participants

common meetings

facilitators

Work groups | Work groups

Finance

Site search

Recruitment & orientation

Outdoor Areas

Energy

Coordinating Group

Orginizing Meetings
• Agenda
• Scheduling

Legal Agreements

Public Relations

Common Facilities

Minutes & Newsletter

Future committee

Organization of committees or work groups during the development process.

- recruiting and orienting new members
- examining needs and desires for common facilities
- examining needs and desires for outdoor areas
- contacting the building department, public officials, architects, etc.
- publishing the newsletter and meeting minutes
- coordinating committees and meetings

Meeting formats vary, but it is important to devise a system where everyone has an opportunity for input without a few people dominating discussions. Small group discussions work well in this respect, as do "round-table" discussions where each person has an opportunity to comment on a topic. The job of facilitating meetings is usually rotated within the coordinating group or within the entire membership. Some communities have found that small groups that meet between common meetings allow for more informal discussions. This format not only allows people to gain a better understanding of the issues and of others' opinions, but it also decreases the need for long discussions during common meetings so decisions can be made more efficiently. Saettedammen had such success with this format during the planning process that the small groups continue to be used today.

Decision-making procedures also need to be carefully considered and agreed upon early in the planning process. Most cohousing groups try to use consensus as much as possible, but fall back on a majority or two-thirds vote when time pressures require a prompt decision. Some decisions may also be delegated to committees.

Goals and Priorities. In preparing the development program, the group must clarify and further define their initial goals, discussing issues in ever-greater detail. The

established early on. One approach is to divide participants into committees (also called work groups) responsible for different areas. The committees may work with consultants on complex issues such as financing or technical considerations, and then present options and recommendations at common meetings where most decisions are made. Typical committee responsibilities are:

- investigating financing options
- investigating energy options (solar, etc.)
- contacting the press and managing public relations

group also needs to agree on priorities. Which shared facilities are most necessary, and which are less important? Which amenities can be done without in order to keep costs down? By its very nature, the design process requires trade-offs; few people can afford everything on their wish list. Establishing the group's priorities early in the planning process assures that participants agree on a basic set of premises from which to make future design decisions.

One inadvertent effect of the cost limitations required to qualify for cooperative financing in Denmark (available since 1981) has been to force cohousing groups to clarify their priorities. Although earlier cohousing groups attempted to keep prices below market rates, many had difficulty designing within their original budgets. Only when limitations were set by an outside source (the Ministry of Housing) did groups succeed in keeping unit sizes and construction costs within their original budgets. Rather than suffering from bureaucratic restrictions, cohousing developments have actually benefited by being required to clarify their priorities.

Consultants. Enlisting the assistance of facilitators, architects, lawyers, and financial consultants who are supportive of the group's goals significantly expedites the development process. An architect or planner can facilitate the initial planning stages by giving an overview of the development process, recommending timelines, and identifying when certain decisions need to be made. Architects also assist groups in clarifying their design objectives and requirements, and in formulating the actual development program.

Consultants familiar with local land and development costs, financing possibilities, and ownership options can assist in defining realistic financial expectations early in the process. Consultants who are themselves committed to the cohousing concept are more likely to provide the nontraditional services required in a participatory process, such as extra meetings, field trips, explanation of options, or facilitation of group decisions. At the same time, consultants must not dictate decisions for the group; this can create a power struggle, and in at least one case caused the firing of an architect.

Sometimes professionals within the resident group can provide some consultant services. While this may reduce costs, it can also create conflicts between the personal and professional interests of the resident consultant, and should be given careful thought beforehand.

In considering how best to use consultants, residents must decide how involved they want to be in various aspects of the process. Whereas most major issues are decided by the resident group, countless technical decisions can be delegated to outside consultants. Communities developed in recent years have felt it less important to be involved in every aspect of development, and tend to give more responsibility to the architect and other consultants than did their predecessors, partly due to increasing economic pressures to keep to a strict timeline. Group involvement in every decision usually takes more time, and therefore costs more than hiring consultants. In addition, Danish architects today have a better understanding of the needs of cohousers. Typically residents play a very active role during the initial planning stages and delegate greater control to the architect and other consultants as the process proceeds.

Development Strategy. The development strategy is often decided by the initiators without exploring all possible alternatives. While groups in the fragile early stages need to be careful not to discuss so many possibil-

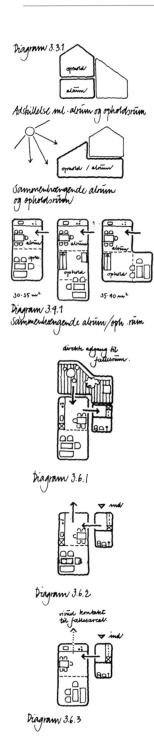

Diagram 3.3.1

Adskillelse ml. atrium og opholdsrum

Sammenhrængende atrium
og opholdsrum

30-35 m²   35-40 m²

Diagram 3.9.1
Sammenhrængende atrium/oph. rum

direkte adgang til
fallesrum.

Diagram 3.6.1

md.

Diagram 3.6.2

visuel kontakt
til fallesareal.

md.

Diagram 3.6.3

Diagrams illustrating spatial relationships for Tinggarden's dwellings.

ities that they never move forward, they do need to consider carefully what is the most appropriate strategy for their particular situation. Will the resident group act as developer? Should they joint venture with an experienced developer? What are the concerns of local officials, and how can the group best accommodate them? Such questions should be asked early on. If, for instance, local officials and neighborhood organizations are concerned about preserving open space, a design that addresses that issue and preserves the natural amenities of the site is more likely to gain their support. Thus the development strategy chosen can help to win the backing of key officials and organizations which can be critical in getting planning approvals.

Design Objectives and Requirements.

Design objectives and requirements make up the bulk of the final program document (outlined earlier in this chapter), and provide the basis for the architectural design, although many other issues are also discussed in preparing a program. An architect can assist the group in discussing these points by laying out the range of possibilities, outlining important considerations, and providing inspiration and resource material. Field trips and analysis of favorite places help to broaden the group's understanding of design characteristics.

A useful tool is a priority checklist on which participants rate their individual design considerations. Building on earlier decisions about goals and priorities, participants identify exactly what functions the private dwelling, the common facilities, and the outdoor areas should accommodate. Is work space needed in some dwellings? Are some households adamant about having their own washing machine? What are the eating, food preparation, and entertaining needs of the private dwelling? Of the common house?

Clearly defining the functions to be accommodated is much more important than assigning square footage requirements, as in conventional programs. In other words, figure out how many to seat in the dining room, or what activities the children's room should accommodate, and let the architect determine how much space different design solutions require. The completed development program formulates these considerations in terms of desired physical characteristics and design requirements and objectives.

Legal Agreements. Before a group can proceed very far in the planning process, it must give serious consideration to its legal organization and individual and shared liabilities. Legal agreements serve several purposes besides settling questions of liability. Requiring members to sign an agreement, even in the initial stages, clarifies who is able or willing to commit to the project —sorting out those who are serious from those who are still curious observers. (Observers may be allowed to participate, but have no vote in decisions until they make a formal commitment.) Becoming a legal entity also inspires confidence among members and consultants alike. Banks and realtors are unlikely to work with a group of people who have no binding agreement among themselves. Finally, a legal agreement clarifies how the building cost will be divided among members.[3]

There are generally three stages at which legal agreements need to be drawn up, reflecting the needs of each development phase. These agreements are: 1) an initial pre-site acquisition agreement, 2) a "building association" or development partnership, and 3) a definition of the final ownership structure and management association.

The initial agreement, drawn up before the group is ready to purchase a site, generally outlines the group's purpose, decision-making procedures, membership recruitment methods and limitations, and fees to cover operating expenses and consulting services. An example of such an agreement appears in the case study of Drejerbanken.

When the group is ready to purchase property and/or hire consultants (architect, lawyer, etc.) for extended services, a more extensive legal agreement is necessary. At this point the group typically incorporates as a building association or development partnership, which functions through the construction phases, and members are generally required to invest a minimum amount toward the down payment on the site and put up collateral to guarantee the construction loan. Danish banks require cohousing partnerships to be liable individually and jointly, so that each member is financially liable for their proportion of the partnership's debts. Banks typically require purchase commitments for at least half of the units before they will approve a construction loan, or sometimes even a site acquisition loan. Those who put up the initial investment for consulting fees and uncommitted shares are reimbursed later from the construction loan. This is a critical stage, in that members are now taking very real risk. Should the partnership decide to dissolve, a portion of the individual investment will have already been spent and could be lost. We should point out, however, that every cohousing community that started construction has been successfully completed and occupied.

Bylaws for a building association or a development partnership are drawn up with the assistance of an attorney, and generally include provisions for:[4]

- the group's general intentions
- membership requirements
- decision-making procedures
- financial liability (individual and joint)

- who can legally represent the association
- members leaving the group[5]
- settling financial accounts when someone withdraws
- amendment procedures

If a group joint ventures with a developer (as in the case of Bondebjerget), the development agreement will reflect the nature of that relationship.

Once construction is completed and the construction loan is transferred to individual or cooperative mortgages, a permanent homeowners' or residents' association and its bylaws replaces all previous agreements.

Design and Construction Documents
Architectural design begins in earnest when a site is found and the development program completed. Each phase of the design process becomes more detailed—beginning with a schematic design proposal, through design development, to completed construction documents detailing how the structures are built. Usually an architect has already worked with the group to prepare the development program, and the design phase continues the process of working with residents to translate their goals and objectives into an actual design. In a few instances, such as Trudeslund, the group had the professional capability to complete the program on its own before hiring an architect. We found in our research that when the organizing group prepared the development program on their own, they typically had a more conventional architect-client relationship—requesting the architect to submit design proposals, rather than working out solutions together with models and other participatory techniques.

In most cases, residents want to be involved in the initial design. Various participatory methods help to promote involvement—questionnaires, models, field trips,

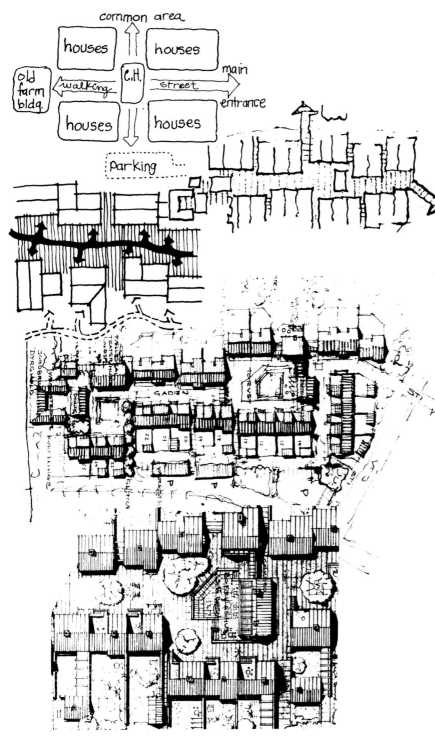

Design development sketches for Bakken (architects: Tegnestuen Bakken).

discussions, and furniture paper cut-outs to develop floor plans are a few. Models with movable pieces, whether of house plans or site plans, and field trips to experience different architectural solutions and building densities are considered the most useful by both architects and residents. Visiting existing housing complexes helps residents understand the consequences of different designs and gives the group and the architect a common frame of reference for design discussions.

More important than specific participatory techniques are the relationship between architect and residents, the cohesiveness of the group, and the architect's ability to translate social goals to a physical environment. If there are unresolved issues within the group, or if participants have not developed an effective working relationship, the architect will have difficulty working with the group. Architects must educate the group about the social consequences of various design decisions and be honest about their own biases; all parties must learn when to challenge and when to compromise. Architect Jan W. Hansen told the participants of one cohousing group, "We will challenge you to try unconventional design solutions. We are not unbiased; but you can say no anytime." This illustrates the difference between residents having input and residents having control.

The work of the firm Vandkunsten, the architects of Trudeslund and Savvaerket, provides an interesting perspective on the relationship between architect and residents. This firm has been an outspoken advocate of both resident participation in design and cohousing. Residents who live in Vandkunsten's projects express great satisfaction with the designs, and in our own research we found that these developments proved among the most effective at translating social goals into a physical environment. Yet both architects and residents recall the design process for these projects as tumultuous. The architects advocated a more radical design approach, fighting for smaller units and fewer private amenities, as well as aesthetic considerations the residents considered unimportant initially. Vandkunsten has gained considerable respect for its cohousing designs—but not because it is an easy firm to work with. The architects confrontational approach forces residents to clarify their priorities and objectives, which produces strong, articulate resident groups.

Other cohousing groups seek architects less vocal about their own opinions and more willing to serve as technicians to draw up the residents' design ideas. Although these groups may have enjoyed making design decisions on their own, in hindsight many residents expressed disappointment in the result. One such case is Gug, where residents designed their own interiors with little input from the architect. Several of the units we saw had basic problems with circulation and layout, which most architects would have foreseen. The architect also offered several alternative site plans, but provided little discussion of their advantages and disadvantages. A resident commented:

He said you can have this or this or this. . . . He should have said, "This is a better solution because. . . ." At the time, we thought it was great, making so many decisions; we didn't want any experts. But we didn't understand then what the consequences would be.

The most effective participatory design processes recognize both the value of resident input, and the professional experience of designers who understand the needs of cohousing groups.

How much influence residents want over the design of their individual residences should be clear from the beginning of the

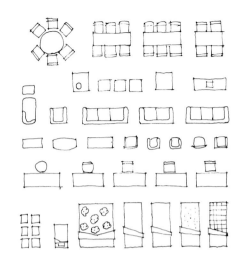

Paper furniture cut-out samples.

design process, since this can have a considerable effect on costs. The greater the standardization of elements, such as interior finishes and kitchen fixtures, the less expensive construction will be. Even when they understand this, participants often have difficulty agreeing on standard choices—after all, most people have the strongest opinions about the interior design of their personal living environment. In retrospect, most residents agreed that individual choice was not so important after all, and they would use more standardized designs if they had it to do over again. One way to accommodate individual taste is for residents to finish their own interiors; see "The Resident-built Option" below.

Participants also recommend leaving most technical and aesthetic decisions to the architect, since it is almost impossible for most groups to agree among themselves on these issues. For example, when architect Jens Arnfred of Vandkunsten suggested painting the interior walls of the Savvaerket common house an intense blue, residents protested, "Absolutely not!" When, after months of discussion, they could not agree on another color, they eventually used the very shade of blue that Arnfred had originally suggested. Attempting to find a compromise agreeable to everyone can be very time-consuming, and generally has not paid off in better choices than experienced consultants provide.

Construction

Groundbreaking is an exciting time for cohousing groups. All the months of planning and long meetings finally begin to take tangible form. This doesn't mean the group can relax once construction starts; complications at this stage can add substantially to the final cost. Major financial and design decisions have been made, but residents still must decide on many details. They must be able to make decisions quickly to keep up with the progress of construction. We heard many stories of difficult meetings where "a decision had to made because they were pouring the concrete the next day." Typically, a "building committee" is delegated responsibility for daily contact with the contractor and architect, and for making quick decisions when the full group does not have time to meet.

The most common mistake at this stage is allowing individual households to make changes during construction. Several communities complained that "the contractor was too nice." Being flexible and allowing residents to change building specifications on site—a different kitchen counter here, an additional door there—complicated the building process and added unanticipated costs. The terms of the construction bid should be carefully worked out beforehand, and no changes should be allowed during construction without the approval of the larger group or the committee monitoring the building process. Residents may swear at the contractor and the committee for not allowing "just this one little change," but in the long run, a firm policy will save the community much grief and money.

The second most common advice we heard about construction was: "Finish the common house first." It is a great asset to have a place to meet, eat, and do the laundry while the houses are being completed and people are moving in. Also, having a functioning common house from the very beginning establishes a pattern of daily use, helping to break the old habits of people who have never had such facilities before.

The Resident-built Option. In most cohousing developments, the residents do some of the construction themselves. In some cases they complete only the landscaping, while in others, such as Sun and Wind, they do much of the interior construction—laying floors, installing cabinets, and finishing walls. In Denmark, exterior walls are usually brick, and interior bearing walls are often lightweight concrete, making it difficult for unskilled residents to build the whole structure. Nevertheless, at Jerngarden and Bofaelleden the residents did extensive renovations of existing buildings. Each project was only eight units, and each group included members with considerable construction experience. In two other communities, Mejdal I and II, residents built the common house after moving in.

The main reason for adopting the resident-built option is to reduce the required cash investment by doing some of the work. The resident-built approach also permits interiors to be customized to fit the aesthetic choices and financial limitations of individual households.

Allowing residents to choose among several levels of finish is one way to accommodate diverse incomes and varying interests in doing construction work. At Bakken, residents chose from three degrees of finish: 1) "maximum resident-built" (a brick shell with a bathroom but no windows, doors, flooring, or ceilings); 2) "medium resident-built" (no

interior doors, stairs, baseboard, or sleeping lofts); or 3) "nearly finished" (no kitchen cabinets or paint finishes). Unfortunately, complications and changes by residents during construction canceled out any cost savings from resident building at Bakken. With stricter construction management, such an approach could be an innovative method for incorporating individual needs and preferences.

Resident construction efforts can take advantage of cooperative work structures already established in the planning and design process. If each household is left on its own to finish its dwelling, as was the case at Gyndbjerg, frustration and resentment can build within the community. By working together, residents share skills, experience, and emotional support. One technique is to work in construction teams specializing in different building skills: Team A paints the interior walls, Team B lays flooring, and Team C installs kitchen cabinets. Residents unable to do construction work can assist

At Bakken, residents finished most of the interiors themselves, including installing the floors, ceilings, and cabinets.

with meals or child care.

Resident-building also has its limitations. Residents must have equity in the project if they are to have an incentive to contribute labor. Although renters have installed landscaping in some rental housing, they cannot be expected to contribute much more than that without financial incentives. Cohousing demands a lot from residents, both before and after construction. Single parents, elderly persons, or time-pressured professionals may not be able to take on the added burden of putting in time on construction. Construction efforts can also take energy from other community activities. At Sun and Wind, finishing the interiors of the houses so exhausted residents that many other community activities did not fully develop until two years after moving in.

To successfully incorporate resident-built activities, groups must be realistic about the trade-offs and how much work the group is ready to do, with careful consideration of financial limitations, construction experience within the group, and how much time residents can contribute.

Participatory Process Is Essential
The participatory development process is not an established, step-by-step procedure; rather, it is a process that requires flexibility and compromise. Every situation is different, determined by the participants, the development strategy, attitudes of local officials, and many other factors. Several additional considerations stand out in reviewing the experiences of Danish cohousing groups.

First, it is important early in the planning process to set a realistic timeline outlining phases and the timing of key decisions. The group should make every effort to stick to their timeline, even though it is difficult, if not impossible, to control outside influences. If the decisions required of residents are made as scheduled, the process will keep

moving forward and there will be less resident turnover during the development process.

Keeping to a timeline means avoiding backtracking. Once decisions have been made at each phase, the group must move on to the next phase. If everyone understands the issues and the agreed-upon solution at the time, old issues are less likely to resurface.

How new members are recruited and oriented also affects a group's ability to stay on track. To retain continuity, it is best not to bring in new members in the middle of a phase, such as the preparation of the development program. Ideally, groups should only bring in new members at the beginning of a new phase of the development process. In actual practice, once the initial program has been set, new members are usually accepted at any time until all units are filled. Recruitment campaigns should be organized at key points, such as before site purchase and before taking a construction loan. New members should be oriented as to the history and status of the group, which decisions have already been made, and which are still open for discussion.

Turnover of participants is an inescapable difficulty of the participatory process. Some families are pressured to find other housing before the project is completed; people may move for job opportunities; and others become discouraged or decide they are not ready for cohousing. In some projects with long planning periods, turnover left only three or four households who had participated from start to completion.[6] However, the number of residents who participate in the entire process does not seem to affect the success of a project once it is completed. The backbone of the project is the organizing group of people committed to it because they intend to live there.

The cohousing development process can

be difficult for everyone, requiring residents and consultants alike to take on unaccustomed roles. Residents must assume greater responsibility (and risk) in determining their housing needs, and in understanding the planning and development process. Consultants need nontraditional skills, such as the ability to work with groups and facilitate decisions, to make technical issues understandable to laypersons, and to consult on the consequences of different choices.

Yet, only through this participatory process have cohousing communities actually gotten built. One resident commented:

Those meetings created an openness between us as we learned each other's strong and weak sides. . . .Without that phase I would not have the same relationship to the common house or the outdoor areas.[7]

The involvement of residents from the earliest planning stages motivates them to take responsibility for the project's success; it allows them to understand the restrictions that must be imposed and the choices that must be made.

Notes

1. Jan Gudmand-Høyer, "Ikke kun huse for folk—ogsa huse af folk" (Not only houses for people—also houses by people), *Information*, (April 4, 1984). The cohousing development process is much easier in Denmark today than at the time Gudmand-Høyer wrote this, so this statement is no longer true. Nevertheless, it is an appropriate assessment of the difficulties cohousing development will face in other countries until it becomes an established housing type.
2. Tarja Cronberg and Erik Jantzen, "Building for People: The Theory in Practice" (Statens Byggeforskningsinstitut, Saetryk 299, 1982): 10.
3. For example, a member's financial investment and obligations cannot be recovered until a new member replaces the outgoing member.
4. See Trudeslund's Building Association Bylawsas an example in the Appendix.
5. *Veje til Bofaellesskab* (Byggeriets Udviklingsråd, 1983), 49-50.
6. Ibid.,14.. In Trudeslund only four of the original initiators actually moved in, but nearly everyone who was a member nine months after the initial meetings moved in.
7. Ibid., 137.

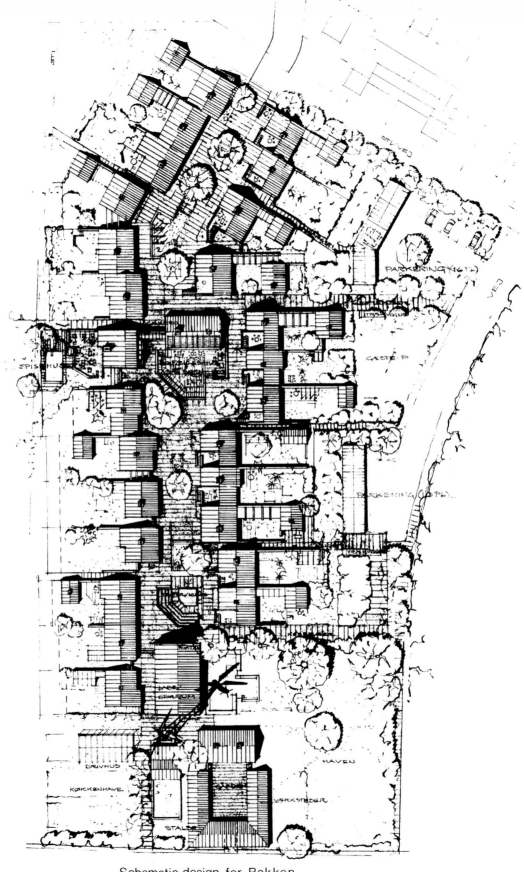

Schematic design for Bakken

No team of architects and planners could be more successful at reducing activity in residential environments than has already been accomplished in sprawling suburbs or apartment blocks.

Jan Gehl,
Life Between Buildings

Design Considerations

While the participatory development process initially creates a sense of community among cohousing residents, it is the design of the physical environment that will support or negate those ties. The environment can promote or discourage interaction between people, resulting in either a lively or lifeless place. Designed to ensure individual privacy, conventional condominium and single-family house developments rarely incorporate design factors that encourage neighbors to meet or that provide children with safe and challenging play areas. As a result, residents of many condominium complexes barely know each other (despite their proximity), and conflicts often arise over children playing in "off-limits" areas. Providing small gardens and comfortable sitting places overlooking shared outdoor areas makes it easier for people to meet their neighbors. We know from our home in California that we have met many neighbors while working in our front garden; without such a garden, that opportunity to interact would not exist.

A considerable body of research now exists that shows how design factors affect people's satisfaction with the places they live. These findings are the basis for design guidelines established in the last decade for conventional housing where future residents are identified only as generic household types (first-time buyers, empty-nesters, etc.). The works of Clare Cooper Marcus, Christopher Alexander, Jan Gehl, Oscar Newman, and others provide excellent references on the social considerations for designing conventional types of housing.

The three topics of this chapter—the site plan, the common house, and the private house—cover specific considerations for the design of cohousing. If we seem to be carried away with encouraging socializing as opposed to protecting privacy, it is because our research has shown that privacy is more readily provided for. Architects tend to give priority to protecting individual privacy rather than creating opportunities for meeting other residents. Yet, of the hundreds of cohousing residents we interviewed, not one complained of lack of privacy, while many could point out design features that discouraged sociability. The design should allow residents to choose whether to be with others or to be alone.

This chapter does not discuss other general issues of good design, such as solar orientation, construction techniques, or choice of materials. These topics are amply covered in other design books.

Cohousing requires special considerations because the residents have chosen it specifically for its strong sense of community, and because they know one another much better than neighbors usually do. People do not generally think about the impact of design on community life, but the social consequences of cohousing design are of particular importance. Cohousing residents must familiarize themselves with these issues as they participate in the design process. Similarly, the architect's role expands to include inspiring members, helping them visualize and communicate their ideas, and providing resource material.

The variety and number of cohousing communities in Denmark provide an excellent opportunity to compare how different design solutions fulfill the social goals of the resident groups. Despite differences among participant groups and their development processes, most cohousing communities began with remarkably similar goals. By comparing these cohousing environments and the testimony of their residents, we can observe how different design solutions resolved similar problems equally well, while others missed valuable opportunities.

The Site Plan

Cohousing has been built in many forms —detached single-family houses, attached row houses, dwellings clustered around courtyards, rehabilitated factories and schools, even high-rise buildings. Theoretically, any form of housing can be developed as cohousing. Cohousing concepts have even been applied to make failing developments more habitable, as in the case of Stakken, the eight-story complex

Vildrosen's site plan clusters 12 detached houses around three courtyards, giving the sense of a small village. An African acquaintance of one of the residents told him that this was the first place he had felt at home in his four years in Denmark because it was organized similarly to his village at home.

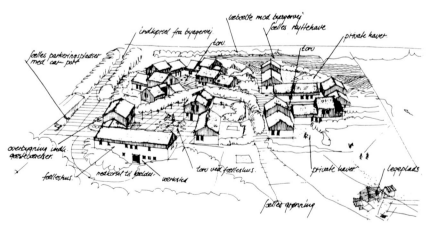

in Gothenburg, Sweden (see Chapter 12 for more on Stakken).

The majority of Danish cohousing takes the form of one-, two-, and three-story attached houses, often referred to as clustered or medium density, low-rise housing. This building type has many advantages over both detached single-family houses and high-rise apartments. It uses land, energy, and materials more economically than detached houses; and the relatively high density of clustered housing also supports more efficient forms of mass transit. While multistory apartments are high density, they are rarely desirable to families with children. Moreover, living more than three or four stories above the ground creates feelings of anonymity in many people.[1]

In rural and semirural areas, clustered housing can help preserve open space, an increasingly sensitive issue in high-growth areas where the demand for housing often conflicts with agricultural needs. The Overdrevet community illustrates how clustering the dwellings preserves much of the land for agricultural and recreational uses, and retains the rural feeling of the site.

Clustered housing can provide many of the amenities of single-family houses, such as direct access to a private garden and an individual entrance for each dwelling. Moreover, grouping the houses together can create larger, more usable open spaces for playgrounds and sports fields. The ability to provide both privacy and community is what makes clustered housing such a popular form for cohousing communities. This chapter will focus on designing clustered cohousing, but similar principles apply to other building forms.

Especially in cohousing, the treatment of spaces between the buildings contributes as much as the buildings themselves to the quality of life. These spaces can be used for sitting, pedestrian traffic, spontaneous

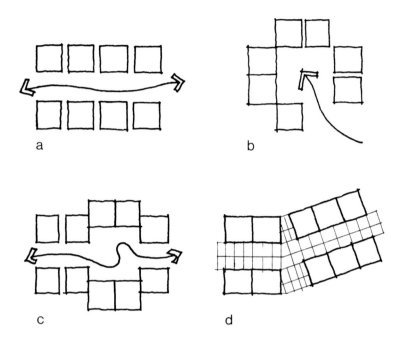

encounters, playing, gardening, and socializing. The site plan, in defining how the site is used, where buildings sit, and how they relate to each other, largely determines how well these activities are accommodated.

Site plans for low-rise cohousing fall into four general categories: dwellings organized along pedestrian streets (Trudeslund, Bakken); around one or several courtyards (Drejerbanken, Ibsgarden); a combination of both streets and courtyards (Sun and Wind); or within one building. (Jernstoberiet, Savvaerket). Some site plans are formal in their organization, while in others, dwellings are situated very informally. With sensitive handling of the relationships between the spaces, all of these site plans can work equally well. Which one the group chooses depends on their goals, the site, and the surrounding context.

Different types of site plans: a. pedestrian street, b. courtyard, c. combination of street and courtyard, d. one building (glass-covered street).

The Ibsgarden site plan uses the traditional courtyard form of Danish farms. The common house is located in a renovated farmhouse originally on the site, while the 21 dwellings are located on the footprint of the original farm buildings. 1. common house, 2. parking, 3. storage sheds.

A Living Place Without Cars. Car access and parking have a major impact on every site plan and are often the first aspects considered in an architectural design. All of the cohousing developments we studied, except for Norgards Plantage, are pedestrian oriented with parking relegated to the periphery of the site. Architect Jan Gudmand-Høyer, who has been working with cohousing since 1964, notes that no matter what the housing type, whenever residents have participated in the design they have restricted cars to the edge of the site. Car-free pedestrian lanes and courts are essential to creating places where small children can play freely and everyone can relax.

Residents may occasionally want to drive to their houses to deliver groceries, drop off a disabled person, or move furniture, but they do not want the cars to be there all the time. One resident exclaimed as he gestured down the pedestrian lane:

The children live here; the residents sit here; the cars live in the parking lot. There is no reason for automobiles to occupy the most valuable area of the site, and lots of good reasons why they should not.

People have clearly stated that they would rather walk in snow and rain than compromise their immediate living environment with cars. Given the harsh Danish winters, this is no small choice!

The primary reason residents give for preferring a car-free site is children's safety. In addition, however, the encounters that occur enroute to the parking area serve an important social function.

People meet in the parking lot going to and from work, arrange car pools, and start friendships through casual chats on the way home. The social life of any neighborhood would be enhanced if cars were parked at the end of the street. Whether parking is centralized or dispersed depends on the site, size, and preferences of the community. Usually one or two centrally located lots are adequate. Using paving blocks or a gravel surface and interspersing trees can even render them attractive. They also make fine play areas for bicycling and ball games during the day when most of the cars are away.

How many cars the residents own typically depends on the site location and the availability of mass transit. Cohousing reduces the need for separate cars since it promotes car pooling and sharing; a family who occasionally needs a second car can easily arrange to share one with another household. Although Danish planning codes typically require a minimum of one-and-one-half or two parking spaces per unit, cohousing developments average considerably fewer cars, often less than one per dwelling. Because cohousers can tell the planning department at the outset how many cars the residents have, they are often allowed to provide fewer than the required number of parking spaces by showing how parking can be expanded at a later date, if needed.

Circulation. Pedestrian circulation can serve as an organizing element for the layout of buildings. Like the main street in a small town, circulation can be organized along a spine, as with a pedestrian lane; or, as in some older cities, it might be focused on a plazalike courtyard.

Circulation to the individual houses from the parking areas and the main pedestrian entrances into the development should be centralized along a limited number of paths to increase the chances for neighbors to pass one another, and to help maintain privacy on the back sides of the houses. Site plans organized around a central street or courtyard work particularly well at promoting such encounters. When houses are scattered around the site, connected by a multitude of

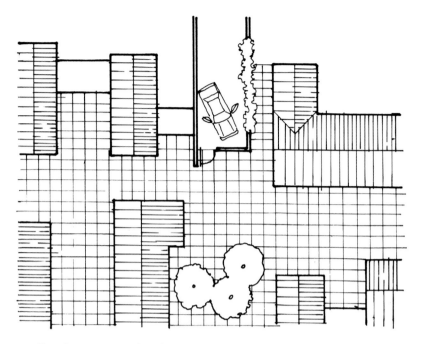

small pathways, as at Skraplanet, no one route gets enough use to ensure the likelihood of meeting others.

Location of the Common House. The location of the common house greatly affects the frequency of its use. For the common house to be an integral part of community life, residents must pass it in the course of their daily activities. Three sometimes conflicting requirements for the location of the common house are 1) that residents pass the common house on their way home; 2) that the common house be visible from each house, or from just outside it; and 3) that the common house be equidistant from all dwellings.

The first of these considerations is the most important. Passing the common house on their way home, residents can see if anything is going on. People stop in to check for their kids, see what's for dinner, or look at the bulletin board. Because the common house is along their path home, visiting it becomes part of their daily routine.

Automobiles are as much a part of our culture as they are a practical necessity. A community car wash area has both practical and social benefits.

The common house at Blahøjen is located so that people will pass it as they enter the community, enabling them to see what's going on inside. Residents often gather at the community plaza in front of the common house on nice afternoons.

Blahøjen site plan: a. parking, b. plaza, c. common house.

Children are the primary users of outdoor areas and consider the entire site theirs to use.

Likewise, if residents can see the common house and its terrace from their own homes, they are more likely to join in when there is activity. One resident told us that he kept his binoculars handy to see if there was anybody he wanted to talk to at the "Friday night bar" in the common house.

Finally, no dwelling should be so far from the common house as to feel isolated, although some residents do prefer to be farther from the action than others.

A Child-Friendly Environment. One of the main objectives of cohousing has been to design "child-friendly environments" that offer many opportunities for play and inter-action. Children in cohousing enjoy more freedom than in other kinds of develop-ments because their playmates live nearby and they know their neighbors well. Since children are the primary users of outdoor spaces, these areas should be designed to accommodate different types of play and to avoid conflicts that discourage their use of the site.

Besides keeping cars at the site's edge, a child-friendly site plan provides centrally located play areas, within sight of the home, for the youngest children. Undeveloped areas invite older children to explore and make up games. In the wooded area behind

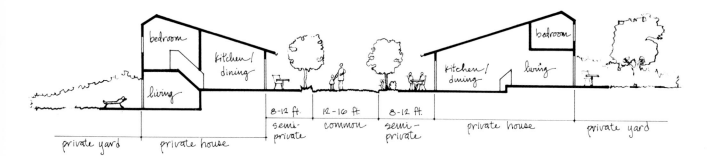

private yard   private house   8-12 ft. semi-private   12-16 ft. common   8-12 ft. semi-private   private house   private yard

the houses at Trudeslund, seven- and eight-year-old boys spend hours with their forts and campfires.

Surfaces for a variety of types of play are also important. Hard surfaces allow for bicycle riding and ball games, while grass is used for rolling or sitting. Children play more on hard surfaces than on grassy areas when both are provided, so plenty of hard-surfaced areas such as wide pathways and courtyards should be provided where playing will not be a problem. Many Danish communities use a thin layer of gravel on walkways, courtyards, and parking areas to provide an inexpensive hard surface conducive to many types of play.

Because children are naturally attracted to activity, they spend a lot of time "hanging out" along major circulation paths. These gathering places should be designed so that the children's noise will not intrude on nearby residences. Possible conflicts between children's activities and the needs of adults can be avoided by considering during the design phase how children will use the site.[2]

Transitional Spaces. The attention paid to the transitions between the private, common, and public realms affect the residents' ease in moving from one to the other, and defines the relationship between the community and the surrounding neighborhood. There should be a hierarchy of spaces, from the sanctity of the private bedroom to the openness of the common plaza. Each transition—from the private dwelling, to the semiprivate front terrace, to the community plaza, to the public realm—helps support community life and relationships among people. If these transitional spaces are not well designed, there will be missing links and fewer opportunities to develop the relationships that make a group of houses into a community. The omission of any of them makes the appropriate use of spaces ambiguous, inhibiting people's activities. These links and thresholds should be indicated physically, although the demarcation can be as subtle as a change in ground cover, or a step up.

Creating a hierarchy of spaces from the most private part of the dwelling, to a semiprivate front terrace, to the common areas, allows residents to choose how private or public they want to be at any given time and makes the transitions between spaces more relaxed.

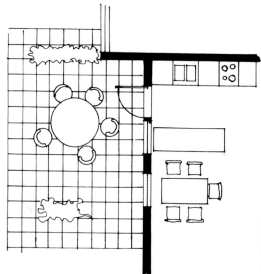

The easier it is to step outside, the more the outdoor space will be used. Corridors, extra doors, and level changes should be avoided.

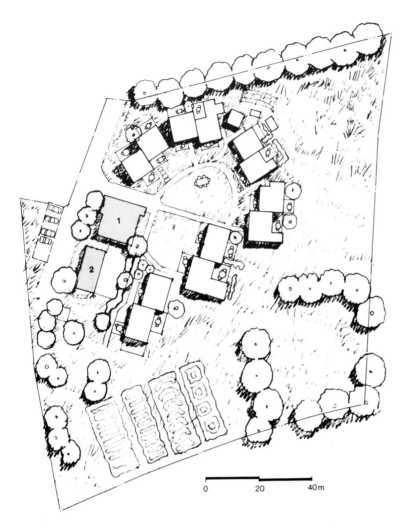

activities. A door and window connecting the private kitchen to the common area allow a parent to watch children playing outside, or to call out to a passing neighbor. Visual access to the common areas, whether they are indoors or outdoors, also allows people to see activities they may want to join. As one resident said, "I can't decide to join the neighbors sharing a pot of tea in the common area if I can't even see that they're there." Casual surveillance is also a highly effective form of building security, with neighbors "watching out for each other" and taking notice of suspicious strangers.

Direct access between the dwelling and a semiprivate garden patio increases the use of outdoor space. When it is easy just to "pop out," people flow between indoors and outdoors many times during the day. This threshold to the common areas is a particularly important element of cohousing. In order to make it as easy as possible to pass from indoors to outdoors, the design should avoid corridors, extra doors, and level changes. If a vestibule is desired for winter entry, a secondary entrance can provide direct access from the living area to the outdoors.

A "soft edge"—that is, a semiprivate area or garden patio between the front of the private dwelling and the common area—further increases opportunities for casual socializing. Urban designer Jan Gehl coined the term "soft edge" to describe "comfortable resting areas, placed on the public side of the buildings and with direct connection to them."[3] Like a front porch where people sit for hours on summer evenings, this semiprivate area provides an easily accessible and comfortable place to be outside and "watch the world go by." Here residents may set out tables and chairs or plant a small garden. Set apart from footpaths by plantings, low fences, or changes in paving, this area need not be large; a space only eight feet deep

Gyldenmuld site plan:
1. common house, 2. guest
rooms and workshop.
Two dwellings (at the lower part
of the site) were located to
maximize privacy. After moving
in, both households wished they
had a more direct connection
to the central courtyard where
many activities happen
spontaneously.

From Private to Common. In cohousing there is less need for territorial definitions, and the relationships between private homes and community areas can be more relaxed than in other housing types. One's front door faces a common area shared by friends, rather than a public street.

This transitional area can support the spontaneous social atmosphere and community life that residents value. Generally, the kitchen-dining area is the room most families "live" in. Locating this room at the front of the house increases opportunities to observe the common area while tending to domestic

The formal entrance of this Trudeslund residence, on the right, leads to a vestibule for winter use, whereas the other entrance on the left provides informal access directly to the kitchen/dining room for spontaneously "stepping outside." The front patio offers a comfortable place to read the paper on a sunny afternoon.

In Galgebakken, a public housing development near Copenhagen, Jan Gehl found the semiprivate front yards were used more than twice as often as the private backyards.

will suffice. In fact, a front yard more than 15 or 20 feet deep will actually deter the flow of activity between the house and the common areas.

A study by Jan Gehl compared outdoor activities in two Danish clustered housing developments. He found that when a soft edge was provided, residents used the area in front of the houses 68 percent of the time that they spent outdoors, compared to 32 percent in the more private backyards. When there was a hard edge and no semi-private area, residents spent only 12 percent of their outdoor time in front.

Even more important, the total number of hours spent outdoors increased fourfold when there was a soft edge. Our findings show that people's preference for sitting or playing in front of their houses is even more pronounced in cohousing: approximately 80 percent of the time people spend outdoors

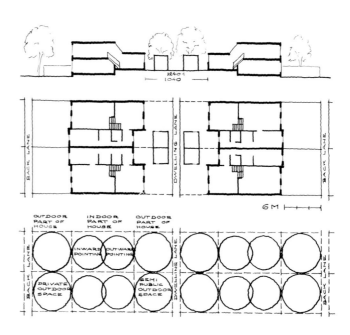

near their residence is spent in the area in front of their own houses, compared to 20 percent in the rear yard. As the "front porch," literally or figuratively, the area immediately in front of the house allows people to observe and take part in community life as they choose.

With interior streets and courts (as at Savvaerket and Jernstoberiet), the transition area between dwelling and common space is reduced and less clearly defined, but it still plays an important role. Not having to worry about putting on shoes or warmer clothing to go outside their residences, people can move even more casually from private to common areas. At Savvaerket, private entrances set back from the covered street provide vestibules for storing shoes, children's toys, and outdoor clothing. Casual

sitting areas along the street are well used all day long.

A private outdoor space is usually provided in the rear of the house, although even here there has proved to be little need for barriers such as fences or hedges. Usually, once residents get to know their neighbors, they find it unnecessary to define territory with fences. In the two oldest cohousing communities (Saettedammen and Skraplanet), fences were dropped from the initial construction for economic reasons. Sixteen years later, only one of the 60 backyards is fenced. Our backyard in California is shared by four houses, making it a spacious and pleasant place. Privacy can be provided with plantings, and if at some point residents need to install fences, they will have a better idea of where and how high they should be.

The two most common mistakes in designing transition areas are providing only a hard edge between the individual residences and the community realm, and placing storage buildings in front of the dwellings. We have seen that a soft transition between the private interior and the common areas encourages informal movement from one to the other, with more time spent outside. Storage sheds are often used for extra household wares, since the dwellings usually lack garages. When these sheds are placed in front of the house, they block views of passersby, children playing, or activities in the common areas. Sheds have even been built in valuable play and sitting areas, and once built, it is difficult and expensive to correct such mistakes. Storage sheds are often better out back. Like fences, residents can build them after moving in, when they better understand how the areas between buildings will be used. Basement storage areas eliminate this problem altogether, but they are not always economically feasible.

Transitions within Common Areas.

The common areas themselves should be designed to provide a variety of gathering spaces—from sitting areas shared by five or six private dwellings to the "community plaza." Again, sensitive transitions from the most intimate to the most public gathering spaces encourage an active community life. For example, along the pedestrian streets at Trudeslund five to eight houses share a picnic table, where neighbors often gather over a pot of tea. On each of the two streets, a sandbox within sight of kitchen windows allows toddlers to play for hours while their parents work or relax with neighbors. Such play areas become meeting places for both children and adults. From the picnic tables and play areas, residents have a view of the common house and patio, where people

---

Body Language

With all of the discussion about designing to encourage casual socializing, the reader might wonder whether a resident can take out the garbage without getting sidetracked. Cohousers told us they quickly learn to use and read body language in various situations. "It's easy enough just to say 'howdy,' and walk on. People know that everyone's busy and has his/her own lives; it's natural and accepted," explained a resident. Body language readily signals approachability. One resident told us that some people may not be approachable for months, because of things going on in their own lives, and then they'll open up again later.

"People in cohousing tend to be very honest with each other," said Finn, a resident for sixteen years. "In my old house, when a neighbor asked to borrow a tool, I felt obligated to loan it, even if I felt uncomfortable doing so. In what might be a rare contact, I didn't want to come off unneighborly. Here if someone wants to talk, or have coffee, or borrow a tool, and I don't feel like it, I don't hesitate to say no. They know me, and there is less likelihood that they will be affronted by my honesty. In fact it's sort of a sign of intimacy to be able to say no."

---

often gather on sunny afternoons.

Some residents expressed concern that local gathering places promote cliques in their communities. Our observations indicate, however, that such gathering places benefit the whole community by bringing residents out into the common areas, and it is only natural that people will become better acquainted with their immediate neighbors. Stopping and resting places should be located where there is the greatest chance that they will be used. Besides benches and tables, low walls and steps also make excellent perches.

Equally important is a community plaza for larger gatherings. When located just outside the common house, as at Blahojen, the plaza functions as the community's "front porch." Here residents gather before and after dinner, have summer barbecues, and hold other community celebrations. Ideally, people should be able to pass by the community plaza on their way home to see whether others are there.

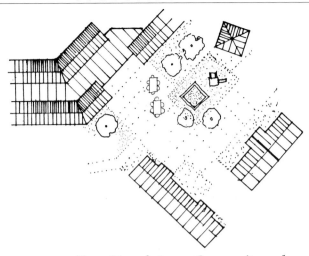

The common house at Handvaerkerparken faces a plaza, which the community shares with the surrounding housing development.

Transitions between Community and Public Areas. Another important transition is between the development itself and the surrounding neighborhood. As members of a tightly knit community, cohousing residents are already set apart from their neighbors in the surrounding area. Insularity can be reduced through the design of the physical boundaries, using such features as shared recreation areas, continuations of neighborhood pathways, or a public plaza. At Sun and Wind, a path used by neighborhood children on their way home from school passes through the site. Trudeslund shares a basketball court with the neighbors. Jerngarden residents painted their houses to blend with the rest of the street; and Handvaerkerparken shares a plaza with the surrounding neighborhood.

Unfortunately, despite cohousing residents' good intentions, their neighbors are not always interested in interacting. When Trudeslund presented its design to the local planning commission for approval, neighbors insisted on a hedge around the site to hide the development. As people learn more about cohousing, there are fewer fears that it will hurt the neighborhood, and links develop more readily with the surrounding neighborhoods. Nevertheless, neighborhood integration at the outset has been a difficult design feature to realize.

The Common House

It's through the activities in the common house that we get to know each other and are able to keep in touch. And that carries over to outside, adding life to the street scene.

Sun and Wind resident

If the single-family house was designed to spread people out across the landscape, then the common house is designed to bring them back together; you could say it fills the gap between the house and the neighborhood. And if it sometimes seems that the single-family house was designed to consume energy, time, and money, then the common house can be seen as a way of conserving all three.

Spatial Relationships. As with the site plan, the relationships between the spaces in the common house—the kitchen/dining room, playroom, workshop—largely determine how well it works. Specific activities, such as attending common dinners, using the laundry facilities, or picking something up from the cooperative store, bring people to the common house, and the design should allow them to see if other people are there. The location and design of the kitchen can be a great asset in this regard, since the cooks are usually working throughout the afternoon and evening. Trudeslund's and Bakken's kitchens are good examples: from any of the common house entrances, one walks by but not through the kitchen, so the cooks know who is coming and going. When the kitchen is closed off from the dining room and circulation (as at Sun and Wind), the cooks are isolated from other activities.

The relationship between the children's play area and the dining area is also important. Although parents want to be within

hearing distance of young children, play areas should be separated from the dining area so the adults can relax after dinner. At Sun and Wind we were surprised to find that residents rushed home after eating, claiming that their small children needed to get to bed. Yet, in other communities with many small children, adults liked to relax together after dinner, drinking coffee and talking while the children played. The difference seemed to be the common house design. At Sun and Wind the play area is directly adja-

cent to the dining room, whereas at Trudeslund the playroom is down the hall—still within hearing distance, but separated from the dining room. The children there can play as noisily as they like while the adults relax. Another community, Gyldenmuld, had a play area at the edge of the dining room. Then the residents built a separate sitting room in one corner; as a resident commented: "It's a grand success; every night we talk and drink coffee there instead of rushing home like we used to."

Residents relax after dinner in Trudeslund's common house while the evening's cooks clean up in the kitchen beyond.

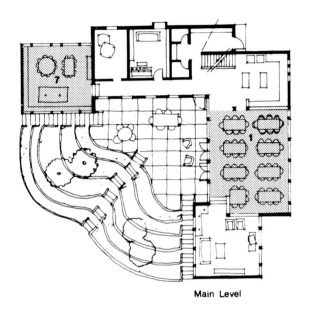

Main Level

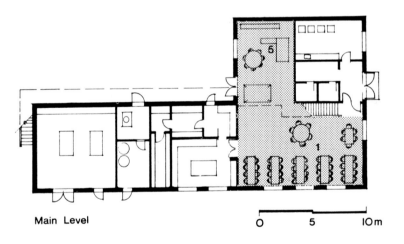

Main Level

0   5   10m

When the children's playroom is directly adjacent to the dining area, as at Sun and Wind, the commotion makes it difficult for adults to relax after dinner. When the playroom is located down the hall, as at Trudeslund, parents are still within hearing distance but the noise is not overwhelming.

Sometimes people go to the common house to get away from people. Late one Thursday evening, a teenage girl was there in leotards, stretching and practicing dance steps; on Saturday morning a lone middle-aged gentleman practiced his saxophone. The common house can also be a place to go just to "get out of the house."

Making the Most of Available Space.
Nearly every community contends that they need a larger common house, regardless of whether theirs is 1,000 or 8,000 square feet. Residents often cite the need for extra guest rooms, which can also be rented out to teenage children or couples having relationship difficulties, or used for work space. Such rooms are now included in many of the new communities. More children's space is also a common request. Building costs, however, limit the space and amenities any community can afford, making it even more important for the design to allow maximum use of what is available.

In many cases, certain spaces are underutilized—the most common example is a separate living room or library. During the planning process residents may envision using the common house like a neighborhood cafe, where they can read the newspaper, relax after work, or meet with friends. But most cohousing communities are too small to sustain that kind of activity. Why make the extra effort to go to the common library to read the newspaper, when one can do it comfortably at home? A casual sitting area, at the edge of the dining room or near the main entrance, takes less space and will be used more frequently than a separate library. People gather there before and after dinner, and are more likely to take advantage of available reading material if they see it sitting out.

Designing for multiple use is one way to take maximum advantage of available space.

For example, the dining room can double as a meeting room. Savvaerket has four 200-square-foot rooms in the common house, which can accommodate a wide variety of uses. Currently two are used for the child-care program, one is a music room, and the other is the teenagers' hangout. "In the future, maybe we'll rent out rooms for a teenager to live in or for someone who wants to work at home," speculates a resident. In addition, four supplementary rooms along Savvaerket's covered street are used as guest rooms or extra bedrooms.

Creating an Intimate Atmosphere. One difficult design problem is to create an intimate atmosphere while at the same time providing for the needs of a large group. The dining room should be comfortable, not cafeteria-like, and there must be places in the common house both for a few people to gather informally and for the whole community to meet. The kitchen should be efficient, with professional facilities adequate for preparing large meals, but it should not be institutional. Cooking and serving should be as convenient as possible, even fun. Visual access between the kitchen and dining area helps to create a residential feeling, as do the choices of interior finishes and light fixtures. For example, using natural wood finishes, rather than paint or plastics, and incandescent lights, instead of ceiling-mounted fluorescent fixtures, help make things cozier.

Some communities have gone overboard to provide a professional kitchen and have consequently failed to create a "homey" feeling. The kitchen facilities at Bakken and Trudeslund allow for efficient meal preparation for over a hundred people, but still have an intimate atmosphere. Our own experience preparing dinners at Trudeslund convinced us that the kitchen's simple design functions very well.

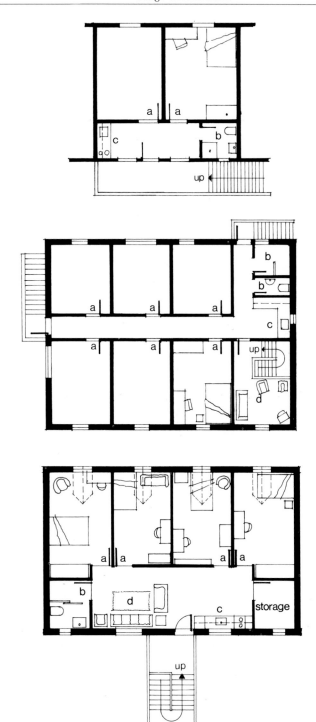

Guest or rental rooms are well used in cohousing communities. Three examples at Drivhuset, Gug, and Thorshammer: a. bedroom, b. bathroom, c. kitchenettes, d. living room.

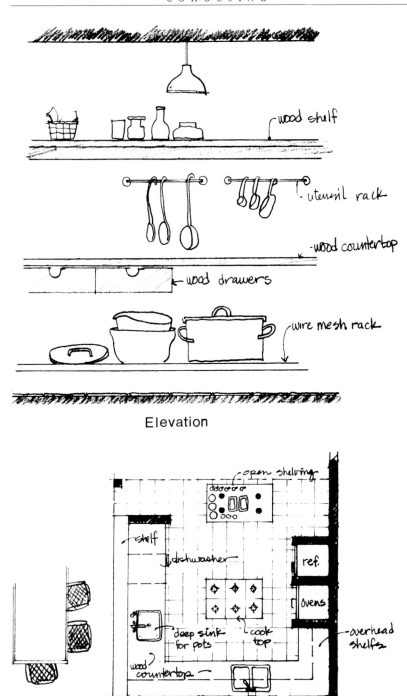

Elevation

Plan

Trudeslund's kitchen is simply designed, but quite adequate for preparing meals for one hundred people.

Acoustics. Good acoustics are necessary to create a pleasant atmosphere. If residents cannot talk in a normal conversational tone during dinner, they are likely to eat at home more often. At Skraplanet, many residents do not eat d'nner in the common house more than once a week because of the uncomfortable noise level; most residents participate in small dinner clubs held in the private houses instead. The flat, hard-surfaced ceiling in the common dining room is the main source of this problem. High angled ceilings and absorbent surfaces help to reduce noise reflection.

Details. Even small details, such as the size of the dining tables, significantly affect the atmosphere. Two communities felt it necessary to have extra-large tables—but then people sit farther apart, so they must talk louder to be heard across the table, which raises the ambient noise level, so that others must talk even louder. A 2-1/2-by-6-foot table, seating six to eight people (including several children), will permit comfortable conversation and promote a relaxed, enjoyable atmosphere. A smaller table or two might be available for families who wish to be by themselves.

The primary purpose of the common house is to supplement the individual house. But it accomplishes much more; it makes a neighborhood a community, and in so doing enhances the quality of life for everyone.

The Private House

Despite all the concern for community and togetherness, people still spend the vast majority of their time in their own houses. As one woman put it, "The beauty of cohousing is that you have a private life and a community life, but only as much of each as you want."

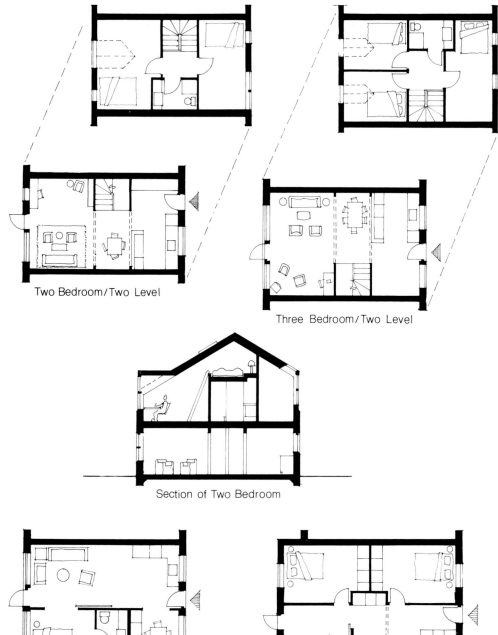

Two Bedroom/Two Level

Three Bedroom/Two Level

Section of Two Bedroom

One Bedroom/One Level

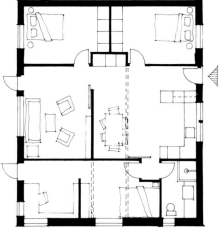

Three Bedroom & Office/One Level

Cohousing communities often develop four or five house models to fit the different needs of participants. Dwellings at Thorshammer range in size from 580 ft² (54 m²) to 1,120 ft² (104 m²).

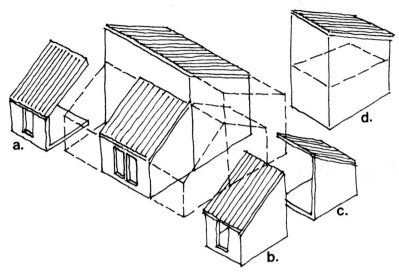

At Bakken, residents could choose to build any number of the illustrated additions initially or at a later date, as their needs dictated.

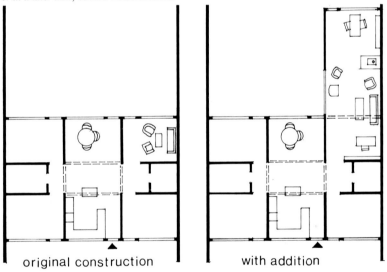

original construction   with addition

Saettedammen's one- and two-story dwellings are designed on a 4 x 3.3 or 4 x 2.2-meter module using post-and-beam construction between concrete bearing walls. This construction method allows for changes and additions as household needs fluctuate. In this example an addition accommodates a home office.

Dwellings in cohousing reflect special design considerations because of the shared facilities, variety of residents, and relationships among residents.

The average size of individual cohousing residences decreased by nearly one-half between 1975 and 1985. Perhaps more significantly, the range of unit sizes became more diverse. At Saettedammen, private residences varied from 1,500 to 1,940 square feet (140-180 m2) when it was built in 1972,

compared to Thorshammer, built in 1985, with unit sizes ranging from 580 to 1,120 square feet (54–104 m2). The average size of cohousing residences built in Denmark today is 895 square feet (83 m2), compared to a national average of 840 square feet for multifamily housing units and 1,389 square feet for single-family houses.[4]

This reduction in cohousing dwelling sizes corresponds to a general decrease in house sizes throughout Western industrial societies, reflecting increases in building and energy costs and declining household sizes over the last decade. In cohousing, the success of the common facilities and strict size limitations for cooperative financing have provided additional impetus for reducing dwelling sizes.[5] With the common house a proven asset that increasingly supplements the functions of the private house, residents are less hesitant to reduce the size of their residences. Space is no longer needed in the home for laundry facilities, guest room, or workshop. Private kitchens have also decreased in size. In Savvaerket, kitchens have only two-burner stoves because residents usually eat dinner in the common house, which can also be used for private parties or formal dinners. The availability of common facilities makes it easier for people who previously lived in larger houses to adjust to smaller units.

Accommodating Diverse Households.
One of the goals of most cohousing groups is to have a diversity of household types and ages within the community. Accommodating this requires a variety of unit sizes and arrangements—including studios, one-, two-, and three-bedroom units, shared houses, and short-term rentals. While several communities have responded to different household requirements by designing each house individually, other design methods are much more economical.

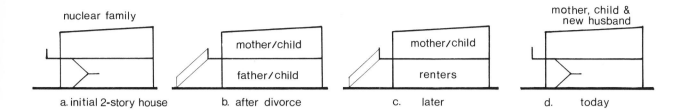

nuclear family   mother/child   mother/child   mother, child & new husband

father/child   renters

a. initial 2-story house   b. after divorce   c. later   d. today

A Choice of House Models. New communities usually devise four to six different house plans for residents to choose from. The basic models are agreed on in the planning process, and those who prefer a specific model work with the architect to refine its design. Individual households often make additional changes (such as alternate kitchen layouts or partition locations) so that every house is slightly different. As we noted in the previous chapter, if not carefully planned for, such "individualizing" can add considerably to the construction costs.

Core Plans. Another way to accommodate different household requirements initially and in the future is to design a core plan with several possible additions, so that one core plan can be adapted to create several different house models. This design method is particularly useful for specifying how later expansions can be made, thus averting potential conflicts among residents.

Accommodating Future Changes:

> *Change is the only constant.*
> Laotse, 6th Century B.C.

Resident stability is important in any neighborhood. If people must move from the development simply because their house no longer fits, the long-range benefits of a stable community are jeopardized. People's lives are rarely static, and neither should their housing be. The birth of a child, children leaving home, divorce, or the death of

a spouse affect a household's spatial requirements. Such events also mark the times when people are most in need of a supportive community.

A variety of dwelling sizes allows residents to move within the community as their needs dictate. Of course, this means that two households within the community must want to exchange at the same time. The ease of exchanging dwellings also depends on the type of ownership. Although rentals or cooperatively owned units are easier to exchange than owner-occupied dwellings, mutually beneficial exchanges between owner-occupiers are still relatively common. "With the help of neighbors, we exchanged houses on a Saturday afternoon. Of course, the paperwork took a little longer," commented a resident.

Flexible Architecture. Flexibility in construction can be provided by designing for future additions (as with core plans), or by subdividing a dwelling into two smaller units. Even when a core plan is not used for the house design, it is useful in the initial design process to allocate area for private expansions and suggest the style and form for additions. The method of construction can also facilitate flexibility. In the community of Saettedammen, the modular post-and-beam construction provided flexibility by allowing the removal of wall partitions and the addition of rooms without compromising the integrity of the structure. Virtually every one of the 27 houses has been altered since the community was completed in 1972. Three

A dwelling adapts as a family's needs change.

189

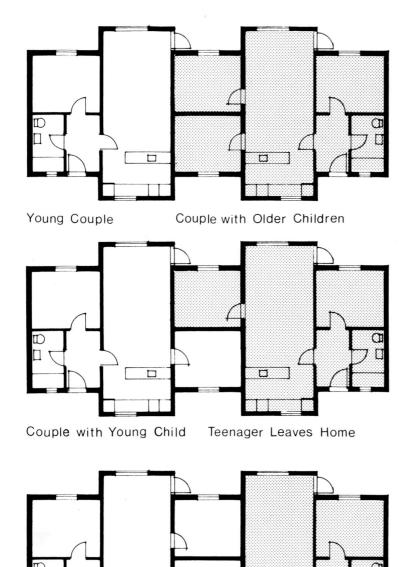

Young Couple Couple with Older Children

Couple with Young Child Teenager Leaves Home

Couple with Older Children Retired Couple

Flexible rooms or "give and take" rooms can be exchanged between the dwelling on either side.

rental room(s)

SECTION

LOWER LEVEL PLAN

UPPER LEVEL PLAN

Bondebjerget floor plan for 1,205 ft² dwelling. Direct access from the entrance to downstairs bedrooms allows teenagers and temporary boarders greater autonomy.

houses have been divided into two dwellings, and four others are now shared by several unrelated people. (The large houses of the 1970s allow more easily for these adaptations than do today's smaller dwellings.) Only five houses were sold in the first 13 years of occupancy.

Another method for accommodating changing needs is to develop architectural designs that can be used in several different ways. In larger houses, the design should allow for the possibility of renting out a room to a student or another adult. Many households can use such rental space to supplement their income during temporary financial difficulties. Renting a room is facilitated by having a separate entrance to one bedroom or direct access from the foyer, so that one does not have to walk through living areas to get to it. This is also an asset for families with teenagers living in relatively small houses.

Another flexible architectural solution is a room that can be exchanged between the dwellings on either side. The Tinggarden development has doors connecting flexible rooms between two dwellings. Residents can very easily close off one door and open the other. Design details to prevent sound travel between units must be carefully considered in such situations. Although the flexible-room design may be more costly at the out-set, it often saves money down the line by allowing people to remain in their homes rather than moving. Limitations on the flexi-ble-room idea include the financial and legal difficulties of exchanges, and the fact that neighbors must have mutually complemen-tary needs to allow for exchanges.

Many communities have found that the most economical and most used flexible space consists of rental or supplementary rooms in the common facilities, such as we discussed under design considerations for the common house.

Designing Small Residences. The small dwelling sizes necessitated by today's econo-my require residents to be more careful in establishing priorities and designers to be more creative in the use of space. It is easy to accommodate many different functions in a large house, but a small house must fit like a glove instead of a grocery bag. In addition to avoiding any overlap with the amenities provided in the common house, residents need to clarify for themselves and the archi-tect what functions are most important for their homes to fulfill. Besides establishing priorities for the allocation of space, resi-dents can also establish priorities for con-

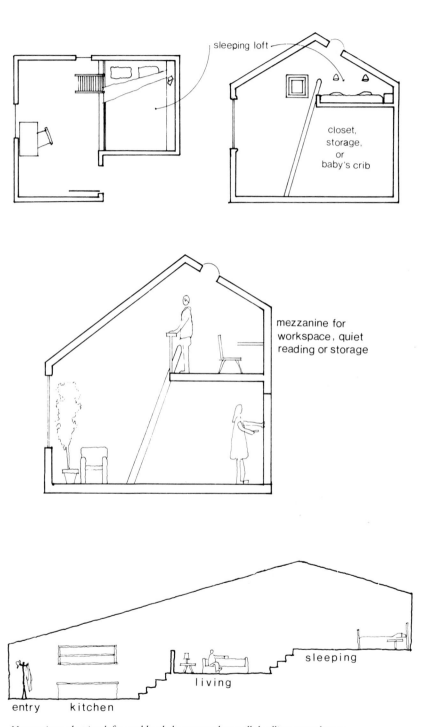

Mezzanines, sleeping lofts, and level changes make small dwellings seem larger.

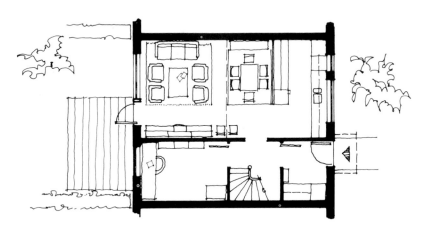

The open floor plan of Andedammen saves space by "overlapping" rooms or borrowing space from adjacent rooms, even if only psychologically. Local lighting, low walls, and/or level changes rather than full-height walls define areas.

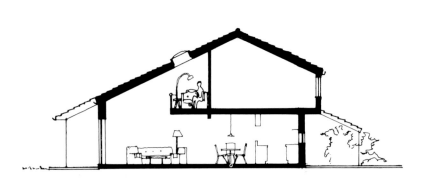

An enlarged balcony with a love seat, coffee table, and reading lamp provides a secondary private space in a scaled down dwelling.

struction quality. Speculative developers may choose to spend less money on sound insulation between units, in order to spend more on quality kitchen cabinets that have more immediate selling impact. When residents are able to make these decisions they are more likely to consider long-term trade-offs, and therefore may choose inexpensive kitchen cabinets so they can afford better sound insulation; kitchen cabinets can always be upgraded later.

The use of sleeping lofts, mezzanines, high ceilings, level changes, light, and the juxtapositions of spaces can help make small areas feel larger. Ceiling heights and window placement can have an enormous effect on how a room is perceived. Making a small house work requires attention to detail. Subtleties add up; acoustics, storage, and even window placement take on greater importance. Design considerations here—how to make the most of little space—are similar to those for all small housing units and are not specific to cohousing.

House Layout. Breaking from the long-held tradition of locating the most formal rooms, typically the living room or parlor, toward the front of the house, cohousers have discovered many advantages to locating the kitchen on the public side of the house, toward the shared outdoor space. This layout creates a stronger link between indoors and outdoors and between private and community areas. It is also much more practical for parents, who can attend to their work or domestic chores while keeping an eye on children playing outside. Conversely, the private side of the house is usually toward the rear or upstairs, where there is as much peace and quiet as in a detached house. A small supplementary sitting/reading area can sometimes be provided in the corner of a balcony or hallway without taking up much space.

Design Issues for a New Housing Type

In this chapter we have discussed design issues of specific importance to cohousing —issues that need emphasis because few people have experienced the unique living situation in this new housing type. We believe that attention must be paid to these issues, to address people's concern about protecting their privacy. Ultimately, the biggest advantage for designers of cohousing is that they can ask the future residents about their desires and priorities. The discussions in this chapter can be used to broaden and direct the dialogue between designer and residents, but should not replace it.

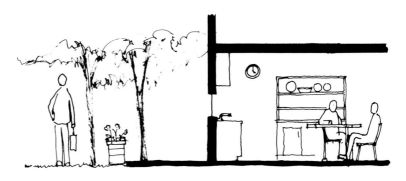

A low window provides good light for the kitchen counter and allows space for cabinets above. People sitting at the kitchen table can see out, but people walking by cannot see in.

Notes:
1. Many studies have compared high-rise and low-rise housing. For more information, see *The Form of Housing,* edited by Sam David (1977); Clare Cooper Marcus provides an excellent bibliography of studies in *Housing As If People Mattered* (1986).
2. See work of Clare Cooper Marcus for more specific guidelines on designing child-friendly environments.
3. Jan Gehl, *Life Between Buildings* (New York: Van Nostrand Reinhold, 1987), 185.
4. These latter figures are 1980 national housing averages, whereas the cohousing unit size average is from developments built between 1984 and 1986. In addition, there are fewer single-person households in cohousing than in other multifamily housing, so these figures are not directly comparable. Nevertheless, they help to place the size of cohousing units in the context of other Danish housing.
5. For any housing development to qualify for cooperative financing, the Danish Ministry of Housing limits the maximum average unit size to 1,023 square feet (95 m²).

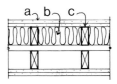

Small construction details, such as sound-resistant walls between dwellings can greatly affect livability. Wall detail: a. double gypsum board each side, b. sound and thermal insulation, c. separated stud wall with air space.

Real Estate

High costs lead to cohousing effort

By Paul Gullixson
Times Tribune staff

Traditional townhouse developments start with some land, blueprints and lots of money.

Judith Steiner's project is working from the opposite direction. "We're starting with the people," she said.

CoHOUSING

When the American-dream model of each family owning a home becomes obsolete

by Kathleen Donnelly

Since she was 12, Marcia Markels has had a picture in her mind of the kind of community she would like to live in. It's like the music and art camp she attended as a child, with a little of the communal living groups she studied in Israel and a bit of the six-flat building she occupied years ago in Chicago thrown in.

In other words, it's a community that's actually c...

Now, ...
local peo...
planning...
help of...
County-b...
idea of "...

Cohousing creates a village in suburbia

By Mary Ann Cook

The way we live now — the nuclear family, the proliferation of single parent families, the mobileness of our society — can be a very lonely way of life. "Most people, if they're honest with themselves, would admit they are lonely." So says educational consultant Peggy Thompson a Monta Vista resident.

But Thompson is one of the few people who is doing something about it. She's part of a core group now forming which is determined to build a cohousing project on the peninsula. The idea is to form a small community with all the advantages of communal living but none of the disa...

"In most condominium developments you start with the developer and end up with the people moving in," says Steiner.

"In cohousing, you start with the people and end up with the developer."

The idea has been successful in Denmark and the Netherlands for about 15 years, says Kathryn McCamant, who works as an architect for Innovative Housing. She and ..., also an architect, spent about ...enmark researching the cohous...d studying how to apply it to ...iving habits. They will present ...tory slide show May 31 at 7:30 ...e Menlo Park City Council ...'01 Laurel Ave.

...n says she definitely feels ...

says. "We need 3 to 4 acres. We could take an existing townhouse, say in Mountain View, and reconstruct it."

In the cohousing concept cars are parked on the periphery of the complex, so that inside the community — it's pedestrian oriented — safe for children and visiting with no traffic or parking worries. A communal center holds laundry facilities, a kitchen, dining room, a recreation room, guest suites, workshop, hot tub and whatever other amenities the group decides is essential. A child care center is usually part of the cohousing setup as well.

Residents have the option of...

HOME
CREATIVE IDEAS FOR HOME DESIGN

Is America Ready For Cohousing?

WITH MOBILITY RISING and households shrinking or fragmented, many Americans are finding a lack of community to be an unfortunate byproduct of contemporary living.

In 1972, the first cohousing development was built in Denmark by 27 families who wanted a greater feeling of community. Now two California architects,

husband/partner **Charles Durrett** found that singles, older people, young couples with kids, single parents and even established homeowners are attracted to cohousing's affordability and sense of neighborhood.

Scandinavia now has over 100 cohousing communities. Though they vary, each combines individual units (including kitchens) with a common house in a pedestrian-oriented environment. In the common house are a

...ican ...ngle-

U.S. ...lear win-the ...ost ...ion, and ...ngle

...liv- ...e an ...the ...of ...ang-

...Menlo Park recently and at-...ed between 75-100 people. ...hompson went to an in-...ational meeting in Feb-...y and has been active ever ... The group meets twice a ...h and "is just about ready

...needed since they are provided in the common area. The same may be true of workshops, garages, teen recreation rooms, laundries and other facilities, depending on the decisions of the group.

Although sizes of households vary, McCamant says the average size of a private cohousing unit in Denmark is about 1,000

away.

"I'm a widow, the kids have just left," Markels says. "I think the way I live is okay, but it's not wonderful.

"I don't always want to have to call people up to make arrangements," she says. "I want to just run into them while I'm picking up the mail and have a conversation."

COHOUSING
Continued from Page 1

Berkeley architects Katie McCamant and Charles Durrett introduced Innovative Housing to the idea after spending more than a year in Denmark studying co-housing. McCamant and Durrett and now writing a book on the subject and serving as consultants to Innovative Housing.

Although Danish and Dutch citizens have already built more than 100 of the communities "it is essentially unknown here," said McCamant. "But people just seem to light up when they hear about it."

CHAPTER FIFTEEN

We have not merely a housing shortage but a broader set of unmet needs caused by the efforts of an entire society to fit itself into a housing pattern that reflects the dreams of the mid-nineteenth century better than the realities of the late twentieth century.

Dolores Hayden
Redesigning the American Dream

Translating Cohousing to the United States

I n the United States, as in Denmark and other industrialized societies, we are experiencing radical changes in family life and work patterns. New forms of housing are not only needed but inevitable, and cohousing is an appropriate and applicable model. While the ideals of individualism and the detached single-family house remain deeply embedded in American culture, changing circumstances are leading many people to question the continuing emphasis on these elements of the American dream.

Reassessing Our Needs

In previous centuries households commonly comprised at least six people. In addition to having many children, families often shared their homes with farmhands, servants, boarders, and relatives. A typical household might include a family with four children, a grandmother or an uncle, and one or more boarders who might also work in the family business. Farmhands and their families often lived in houses clustered around the main farmhouse. Relatives usually lived nearby. These large households provided both children and adults a diverse intergenerational network of relationships in the home environment. Relatives, servants, and boarders assisted with the burdens of parenting, domestic chores, and caring for elders and the sick. The idea that the nuclear family should live on its own without the support and assistance of the extended family or surrounding community is relatively new, even in the United States.

The average size of the American household continues to decline: from 5.8 in 1790 to 4.8 in 1900, to 3.5 in 1950, to 2.6 in 1985.[1] The number of single-person and single-parent households has increased dramatically. Meanwhile the surge in housing and living costs has placed increasing financial demands on these smaller households.

In addition, the majority of women now work part or full time outside of the home, including 52 percent of mothers with children under the age of six. A child-care crisis has resulted, along with an increasing dependence on restaurant and pre-packaged dinners, and a chronic time crunch as households attempt to cover the domestic services once provided by a full-time homemaker on top of their other jobs.

Today's small households are just as likely to be composed of single parents or single adults as they are to be composed of nuclear families. To expect that these households should be self-sufficient and without community support is not only unrealistic but absurd. Each household is expected to prepare its own meals, do its own shopping, and so far as finances permit, to own a vacuum cleaner, washing machine, clothes dryer, and other household implements, regardless of whether the household consists of two people or six, and whether there is a full-time homemaker or not.

People need community at least as much as they need privacy. We must reestablish ways compatible with contemporary American lifestyles to accommodate this need. Cohousing is one possibility.

In many parts of the country, affordable housing is a critical issue. In today's market conditions, government subsidies and financial assistance are usually necessary to make new housing affordable for low- and moderate-income households. The cohousing approach by itself will not reduce housing prices which are largely determined by the costs of land, labor, materials, and financing. Nevertheless, it does offer innovative ways to reduce day-to-day living expenses and reapportion construction costs to reflect the priorities of the residents. For instance, we find many cohousing groups are willing to accept less expensive finishes (which they can upgrade later) in order to afford higher quality exterior materials in windows, insulation, and exterior siding.

Features typical of cohousing design, such as restricting parking to the site's periphery so that less paving and fewer storm drains are required, also reduce some development costs. The organization inherent in cohousing communities makes it relatively easy for residents to work together to do some of the construction and landscaping work themselves. While individual units are generally reduced in size to allow for the common facilities, these facilities enable residents to use many more amenities than most households can afford on their own. Cost-of-living expenses are further reduced by such features as common laundry facilities, dinners, and child care.

While technological advances are making it more common for people to work part or full time at home, working at home often creates further isolation. If the home is to be a viable workplace, it must be restructured to provide for a broader range of social and practical needs.

Crime and violence in American cities have become commonplace, and people in urban areas live with the constant fear of being robbed or assaulted in their own homes. The successful national "Neighborhood Watch" program is based on the premise that the most effective deterrent to crime in residential areas is to know your neighbor and to look out for one another. Cohousing emphasizes building strong neighborhoods instead of building strong security gates.

The suburban sprawl of single-family house developments has long been attacked for its massive consumption of land and energy. Most planners recognize the environmental benefits of higher-density multifamily housing, such as preservation of agricultural land and open space, and facilitation of effective mass transit. Yet, if they offer nothing more than a smaller version of the private house, such high-density developments cannot compete effectively against detached houses for potential buyers. Thomas Cook, Director of Housing and Land Use for the Bay Area Council in San Francisco, believes that the cohousing concept makes multifamily housing more attractive by offering home buyers advantages they cannot get in a single-family house.

In the interest of protecting our individualism, Americans have become starved for community. As early as 1835, the French political writer Alexis de Tocqueville warned Americans in his book *Democracy in America* of the need to balance their individualism with an active involvement in common concerns.[2] More recently, sociologist Robert Bellah and his colleagues argued in *Habits of the Heart* that our individualism has become unbalanced, creating a culture of separation which, if left unchecked, will "collapse of its own incoherence."[3] Increasingly we hear that we must remedy the isolation and loneliness of our culture through a renewed commitment to community.

Cultural Considerations

The present mobility of the American population calls into question our ability to make community commitments, and hence our potential for developing cohousing. Social ties are absent in most neighborhoods today, proving little incentive for people to stay. On the other hand, when a home is tied to a community and to relationships that are valued, people have stronger reasons to move less frequently. One Danish cohousing resident remarked, "Before living here [in cohousing], I found the jobs I wanted and then moved. Now I look for the jobs near here."

The very transience of our culture is one reason why we need new ways of establishing community ties. People who live in the town where they were raised build up a social network over the years. But many Americans live hundreds or thousands of miles away from their families, and have moved numerous times. Cohousing allows people to establish a sense of community relatively quickly, compared to the years or generations it might otherwise take.

Our multicultural society presents unique challenges for the development of cohousing. As members of a more homogeneous culture, the Danes share many traditions, values, and expectations that create an immediate cohesion not readily attainable in the United States. Within the diversity of the American population, however, many people share the basic values needed to live together successfully in cohousing: an appreciation of the benefits of community and a willingness to work together to achieve them. As in Denmark, different cohousing communities in the United States will reflect different values and levels of commitment. Although it may require greater effort to establish shared values and clarify expectations, the cultural diversity of the United States should provide the opportunity for anyone interested in cohousing to find a group they can live with.

A related concern is that cohousing might further emphasize already existing American patterns of residential and social segregation. Certainly cohousing could be applied as just another variation on the walled-in, planned communities of the affluent; but such exclusivity runs counter to one of the primary reasons for the concept's appeal—the desire for an integrated residential environment. In Denmark, cohousing groups consistently "seek a varied resident composition with diverse incomes, interests, and political perspectives . . . encouraging an attitude of openness and tolerance."[4] They also make special efforts to integrate their community into the existing neighborhood. Cohousing groups now forming in the United States voice similar goals as they grapple with issues of affordability and diverse priorities. Cohousing offers an opportunity to overcome the current patterns of segregation by interest, age, income, race, and household composition that these people deem undesirable. In choosing cohousing, residents choose to respect each other's differences, while building on their commonalities.

Building on Past Traditions
Americans have a strong tradition of organizing locally to solve problems, whether in the Pilgrim settlements and pioneer towns of the

past or in the neighborhood organizations and grass-roots political movements of today.

Thomas Jefferson spoke compellingly of the importance of direct citizen participation in governing society and the benefits of decentralized decision making. Even today, when so many Americans are politically apathetic and distrustful of government, our republican tradition is idealized in the town meeting, where residents meet as equals to discuss issues and determine what they will do about them. As a small-scale model based on local initiative rather than government policy, cohousing is especially applicable to the American context.

A Renewed Interest in Community
Throughout the United States there is already a renewed interest in community. Alvin Toffler writes in his book *The Third Wave,* "Everywhere we find a new concentration on 'community' and 'neighborhood,' on local politics and local ties."[5] The authors of *Habits of the Heart* write, "The profound yearning for the idealized small town that we found among most of the people we talked to is a yearning for just such meaning and coherence."[6]

Interest is also growing in various forms of housing that incorporate shared facilities and offer a stronger sense of community. One example is a group of unrelated people sharing an existing house, an option which is becoming increasingly popular among singles of all ages, including single parents. Yet, shared houses have limitations for families and individuals who want greater autonomy than this option provides. Cohousing fills the gap between shared housing and single-family houses, combining the advantages of an intergenerational community with the autonomy of private dwellings.

Shared facilities are being incorporated into other types of housing as well. Planned retirement communities often include shared dining and other common spaces. Congregate housing for the elderly, in which private rooms are organized around shared living spaces, is another increasingly common housing type. And, although only a few examples have been built, housing for single parents with on-site child-care facilities has been very successful. Willowbrook Green, a recently completed development in Los Angeles, combines child-care facilities with 48 rental units. Resident participation in design and management have proven valuable in all types of development. In Santa Rosa, California, a Quaker group initiated a 27-unit cooperative called Santa Rosa Creek Commons, which includes a common meeting room and outdoor space. Participating in both development and ongoing management, residents of different ages, incomes, and religions have created a strong community feeling. Across the country, nonprofit organizations representing a wide variety of constituencies are advocating the development of intergenerational housing with shared facilities. Such projects are becoming more accepted by bankers, planners, and housing professionals. Cohousing communities build on these precedents.

Getting Started in the United States

Our experience in introducing the cohousing model to American audiences confirms that there is broad interest in this housing alternative. Because the public cannot demand what it has not yet conceived, our initial efforts have focused on "getting the idea out" through introductory slide presentations about the concept. In the past three years, we have delivered over one hundred presentations to a wide variety of audiences, including the general public as well as housing and planning professionals. The overwhelmingly positive response indicates that many Americans feel a void in the available

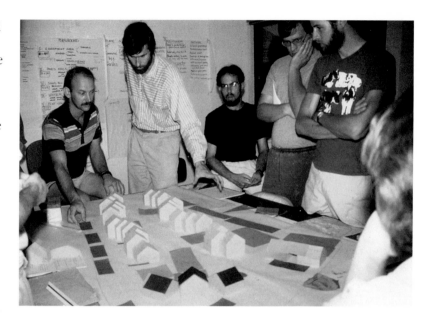

A resident group works with the authors on the design of their cohousing community.

housing options. People of all ages, incomes, and lifestyles are attracted to the social and practical aspects of cohousing communities. We find they are particularly attracted to the intergenerational aspect of these developments. While affordable housing is an important issue, most people's primary interest is clearly the creation of housing options that provide a stronger sense of community.

To facilitate the formation of cohousing resident groups, we have created a series of workshops and offer a national, computer-based referral network. Our "Getting Started" workshop provides participants with an overview of organizing and planning a cohousing community with emphasis on the steps necessary to prepare for site acquisition. This intensive weekend workshop builds momentum tempered with the realities and difficulties of real estate development and gives participants direction in tackling the process ahead.

In the past several years, we have given dozens of these workshops, all of them resulting in the formation of cohousing groups. Most of the workshop participants share similar goals, the major difference being a preference for an urban or a rural setting, or other geographic preferences. (In Denmark also, the issue of site location was a major factor in determining the composition of groups.) Particpant's concerns tend to focus primarily on two issues— financing and their ability to work together. Apprehensions about money are to be expected whenever people consider investing in property. As they become more familiar with the financial possibilities and with each other, these concerns diminish.

By the fall of 1989, 27 resident groups were meeting to plan their cohousing communities and the seeds of many others were being planted across the country. Several groups are now negotiating for sites. Most of these groups are on the West Coast where our work has focused.

Several groups have found it advantageous to initially form "umbrella" groups. A regional umbrella group enables its members to explore local options and get to know others who share their goals and priorities. In addition, the group can generate interest, educate local officials, build community support for the concept, and share experiences and information. From such umbrella groups specific organizing groups coalesce around specific sites or goals.

While many people believe it would be easier to organize a community with friends, we find the opposite is true. When a group forms for the sole purpose of developing a cohousing community, other issues regarding friendships and alliances are less likely to intrude, although initially it may take more time to get to know each other. Groups of friends seem to have difficulty in agreeing on timing and location. They also may have greater difficulty in recruiting new members because people fear being the "outsider" in a group of long-term friends.

Clearly, the most awkward stage for these emerging groups is the period between their formation and pinpointing a specific site. It is difficult for groups to maintain their focus on the steps necessary to prepare them to take action as a cohesive, organized group. Yet, in order for the group to proceed (and be taken seriously in the development world), it is critical that they take this time to build an effective working structure, explore shared values, and sharpen their group process skills. Once a group chooses a specific site, the development process creates its own momentum to keep the group on track. However, if it is not a cohesive group that knows how to work together and has clearly defined its goals, proceeding with a site acquisition or making the financial commitment necessary to acquire needed professional services will be difficult. With the help of our cohousing workshops, many of these first American cohousing groups have suceeded in forming effective organizations that incorporate a diversity of people.

Potential Obstacles
Despite these promising prospects, barriers to developing cohousing remain—the conservative biases of financial institutions and planning departments, legal and liability issues, and general skepticism about a new idea. These problems, though very real, áre not insurmountable. Cohousing communities can use well-established ownership structures such as condominiums, cooperatives (regular or limited-equity),[7] or rentals owned by nonprofit organizations. In fact, resident participation in the development process can help to overcome the management problems that plague many condominium associations.[8] Most condominium residents have had no training in the complex issues of management. In cohousing communities, residents' involvement in the development process provides a training forum for ongo-

ing management. The first American cohousing groups must convince banks that they can handle problems of long-term management; once a number of cohousing developments have proven this, financial institutions may actually prefer lending to them. Obtaining construction financing will also be difficult for the first cohousing groups in the United States where banks are used to working with developers with track records and substantial financial collateral.

Planning departments are already accustomed to working with planned-unit developments, a legal and design concept which allows a development to be planned as an entity, grouping dwellings into clusters and preserving open space. The community rooms and shared amenities in condominium developments establish a precedent for the cohousing common house. By adapting portions from the contracts for housing cooperatives, condominium associations, and Danish cohousing communities, we are working out legal agreements to encompass different stages of the development process and to outline shared and individual responsibilities.

Resident participation in the development process is practically unknown in the United States. Few architects or developers are prepared to work with resident groups and even many of the particpants are concerned about the group process. In our work with cohousing groups we emphasize how members can improve their ability to work together. As we saw in Denmark, working effectively as a group is an ongoing learning process. As facilitators, we have developed programming and design processes that emphasize consensus-building from within the group while keeping to an efficient timeline.

Another potential hindrance is the temptatin to try to build cohousing without resident participation. While this is certainly

possible, residents are unlikely to use the facilities to the extent that they do in cohousing communities. In this case, tenant selection and management efforts will be critical in encouraging their use. Our research consistently shows that when residents are not involved in the planning process, they use the common facilities less frequently, rarely organize common dinners, and usually require outside assistance in management.

The first cohousing developments in the United States will have to overcome many obstacles and much skepticism, but those who believe that the benefits outweigh the difficulties will make cohousing possible. After all, similar barriers initially existed in Denmark.

The CoHousing Company

In 1989, we formed The CoHousing Company, a development company to assist groups in overcoming the barriers to building their cohousing communities. By bringing together a team of real estate and development professionals, we are able to offer a comprehensive package of services specifically tailored for cohousing groups and the participatory process. We provide services in the areas of group formation and facilitation, site search and acquisition, real estate brokerage, land development, design, project management, and finance. The CoHousing Company works with resident groups through the entire development process, from the "Getting Started" workshop to the ongoing management of the community.

Concluding Thoughts

Cohousing is as much a process for developing housing as it is a new housing type. The examples in this book illustrate how ordinary people can organize to build housing that truly addresses their needs.

The cohousing model is a major contribution to Western society's concept of home and community. Yet it clearly has its limitations. At an average size of 15 to 35 units, cohousing developments have limited impact on larger urban and regional design issues. Cohousing may begin to reintegrate work and housing, for instance, but the creation of livable city centers and more efficient transportation systems must be undertaken on a larger scale. Realizing the goal of providing good, affordable housing for all Americans will require a commitment from government and society as a whole. In the meantime, more informal approaches are necessary. Cohousing communites are one model.

We have already learned much about adapting the Danish cohousing model to an American setting and we will learn more in the coming years. But we have noted striking similarities. When workshop participants explain their interest in cohousing, their comments are almost a direct translation of what we heard from the Danes. People speak of their frustration with the isolation of current housing options, the desire for a spontaneous social life that doesn't require making appointments with friends, wanting more contact with people of different ages, and the need for a better place to raise children. These words echo what we have heard from Americans all across the country—not just single parents and seniors, but also young families, professionals, and established homeowners. Clearly, many people are seeking alternatives not provided by the conventional housing industry, and some are ready to do something about it. We hope this book will provide the inspiration and the rudimentary tools for such people to take decisive steps toward a creative solution.

Notes

1. F. E Krobin, "The Fall in Household Size and the Rise of the Primary Individual in the United States," in *The American Family in Social-Historical Perspective,* ed. M. Gordon (New York: St. Martin's, 1978); 1985 U.S. Census Bureau.

2. Tocqueville, who helped to coin the term individualism, traveled throughout the United States in the 1830s seeking to understand the nature of this new democratic society. His book is generally considered one of the most insightful analyses of American culture.

3. Robert Bellah et al., *Habits of the Heart: Individualism and Commitment in American Life* (Berkeley: University of California Press, 1985), 281.

4. Taken from the Trudeslund development program, written by the resident organizing group in 1979.

5. Alvin Toffler, *The Third Wave* (New York: Bantam Books, 1980), 299.

6. Bellah et al., *Habits of the Heart,* 282.

7. Different states have different requirements and limitations on cooperatives. In California, for instance, new housing cooperatives are limited-equity meaning that the equity on the resale of units is limited to an annual appreciation set by law (currently 10 percent), in exchange for public subsidies which reduce down payments and make the price more affordable.

8. Stephen Barton and Carol Silverman, at the Institute of Urban Policy and Regional Development, University of California at Berkeley, have done extensive research on the management of condominiums.

THE AUTHORS

Kathryn McCamant and Charles Durrett are a husband-wife design team with backgrounds in architecture and environmental design. They have formed a development company—*The CoHousing Company*—specifically to build cohousing communities. Together with other professionals they work with resident groups through the entire development process. The CoHousing Company provides services in the areas of group formation and facilitation, site search and acquisition, real estate brokerage, land development, design, project management and finance, as well as providing design and consulting services nationwide. The authors also offer slide presentations, workshops, and a national, computer-based referral network to facilitate the formation of cohousing groups.

Charles has a professional architecture degree from California Polytechnic University in San Luis Obispo and Kathryn holds a degree in architecture from the University of California, Berkeley. Charles worked previously for the San Francisco Mayor's Office of Community Development where he designed child-care facilities. He has also worked independently as a designer as well as for several private architecture firms where he designed dozens of clustered housing projects and many detached houses. Kathryn's background is in nonprofit housing development, specifically working with residents in participatory design and construction projects, as well as traditional architecture.

The couple is currently seeking sites for their own cohousing community. They would like to hear your comments on the book and on the topic of cohousing communities. They can be reached by writing:

The CoHousing Company
48 Shattuck Square, Suite 15
Berkeley, California   94704

Cohousing is a trademark of McCamant & Durrett. All rights reserved. Contact McCamant & Durrett for permission to use the term.

For those who are interested in visiting cohousing communities, please keep in mind that these places are people's homes, not housing exhibits. If you wish to visit the communities, we suggest contacting the association of cohousing communities to make arrangements. Write to:

Lansforeningen af
    Bofællesskaber
Hans S. Andersen
Trudeslund 2
3460 Birkerød,
Denmark

In the Netherlands write:

Centraal Wonen
Bentismaheerd 19
9736 EA Groningen
The Netherlands

Community name and location listed according to general geographic area.

Zealand

(community)	(town)
Andedammen	Birkerød
Bakken	Humlebæk
Farum Midtpunkr, Blok 12	
	Farum
Damgården	Albertslund
Egebjerggård I, II, II,	
	Ballerup
FB-Østerhøj I, II, III	
	Ballerup
Højtofte	Holte
Ibsgården	Roskilde
Jernstøberiet	Roskilde
Hestkøbvænge*	Birkerød
Karolinelund*	Hundested
Kilen*	Ballerup
Kirstinvang IV	Ballerup
Klinteby	Faske Ladeplads
Lerbjerg Lod	Hillerød
Lærkebo*	Vanløse
Låddenhøj	Roskilde
Marklodden	Måløv
Nørgårds Plantage	
	Værløse
Otium*	Birkerød
Savværket	Jystrup
Slagslunde	Stenløse
Skråplanet	Vaerlose
Sneglebo	Roskilde
Stakken*	Jerslev
Stavnsbåndet	Farum
Stejlepladsen	Holbæk
Sættedammen	Hillerød
Tinggården I	Herfølge
Tinggården II	Herfølge
Tornevangsgården	
	Birkerød
Trudeslund	Birkerød
Tubberup Vænge	Herlev
Vaningsstedgård	Karlslunde
Virumgård	
Vodroffvej	Frederiksberg

Æblevangen	Smorum
Økologisk Landsbysamfund*	
	Hundested
Østerhøj*	Østerhøj
Åbakken	Strøby

The Island of Fyn

Bondebjert I,II,III,IV	
	Odense
Drejerbanken	Vissenbjerg
Bjørnemosen	Odense
Blangstedgård*	Odense
Højby*	Morud
Villestofte*	Odense
BOF	Odense

North Jutland

Andelsbyen*	Skive
Andelsboliger med Landbrug*	
	Viby
Askebakken	Nørresundby
Blåhøjen	Aarhus
Andelssamfundet*	
	Aarhus
Asgård*	Skive
A 70	Sporup
Bofælleden	Beder
Drivhuset	Randers
Frugthaven	Skørping
Grusgraven	Hinnerup
Grønmosegård	Skødstup
Gug	Ålborg
Gyldenmuld	Skanderborg
Højager*	Aarhus
Højvang	Randers
Håndværkerparken	
	Højbjerg
Jerngården	Aarhus
Kamillelunden*	Viby
Lynghoved*	Ry
Mejdal I	Holstebro
Mejdal II	Holstebro
Midgården	Beder
Milepælen*	Beder

Møllegården	Mårslet
Nonbo Hede	Viborg
Nova*	Horsens
Overdrevet	Hinnerup
Projekt Landsby*	Ålborg
Snåstrup Mølle	Beder
Sol & Vind	Beder
Stautrup I & II	Rahøjvænget
Tingstedet*	Gullestrup
Thorshammer	Skive
True Byvej	Mundelstrup
Uldalen	Nørre Sundby
Vadestedet	Ry
Vejgård Bymidte	Ålborg
Vidjekær	Skanderborg
Vildrosen	Beder
Ådalen I* & II*	Randers

South Jutland

Abildgården	Bjert
Fladengrund	Esbjerg
Gyndbjerg	Bjert
Kolbøtten	Aabenraa
Solfang*	Fredericia
Vestenvinden*	Ribe
Børkop*	Vejle

* refers to communities planned or under construction.

The following is a translation of the legal agreement between members of a Danish cohousing organizing group (the Trudeslund group) which was drawn up when the group made a purchase offer on the building site. The building association formed with this agreement provided the organizational and legal basis for the planning period. It is included only for the reader's general information. Cohousing groups should consult an attorney about appropriate legal agreements for their situation.

Building Association Bylaws for Boligfællesskabet Trudeslund

(The Cohousing Community Trudeslund)

We the undersigned establish on this date the following building association.

The association's name is:

"Boligfællesskabet Trudeslund"

The association is based in: Birkerød County

The association's address is:(mailing address of one of the members or P.O. Box)

The association's purpose is to acquire the property which is described as Area B in the Local Plan number 7, accepted by the Birkerød City Council on September 29, 1978. The area is defined as an area of 15,940 square meters (3.94 acres).

In addition, the association's purpose is to develop on this site a community for the member's own residence which is envisioned as 33 residences with 1 common house.

Article I

In connection with submitting a purchase offer on the property to Birkerød County, the association has prepared schematic designs for the site plan and house types.

If an agreement to purchase the property is entered into with the county, the association will proceed with preparation of a detailed site plan which can form the basis for the passing of a supplemental development plan. Henceforth the association takes over the property: either the association takes deed to the whole property and thereafter commences to parcel out and pass on the deed to the individual members, or the individual members immediately take deed to each parcel with a share of the common areas, according to arrangement with Birkerød County as the property seller.

Furthermore, the association will prepare a developement program which will form the basis for design development, the authorities' approvals, and bidding.

Article II

The total number of shares in the association equals the total number of dwellings to be built and therefore, at the present, is 33.

One share ascribes to the same privileges and obligations even though more than one person subscribes to the share.

At the time the property is transferred, for every share a minimum sum of 20,000 Danish Kroner (approx. $2500) of one's own capital is to be contributed . The payment is to be paid upon request to the association's lawyer and deposited in an accredited financial institution.

For the association's operating costs during the planning period every share contributes 500 D.Kr. (approx. $65).

Article III

Externally the members are liable personally and jointly opposite third parties for the association's accumulated obligations.

This mutual liability is proportional.

The individual member's share in the association can be used for expenses or other kinds of execution of the association's unauthorized debts.

Article IV

If a member wishes to withdraw from the association, he/she is only freed from his/her obligations when a new member approved by the association's council has joined the association by signing the existing bylaws.

The association can as necessary pass more explicit procedures in connection with joining and withdrawing--and establishing a waiting list.

Article V

The daily work of the association is directed by a council of at least three members.

The council chooses its own chairperson and decides for itself on rules of procedure. Minutes shall be taken for each of the council's meetings and negotiations, and sent to all members as quickly as possible.

The council's decision's are made by majority vote. The council can make decisions when all three members are present.

The council will frequently call membership meetings in which direction for the council's work will be set. One council member or three regular members can likewise at any time, with eight days notice and a proposed agenda, call for a membership meeting for discussion and decisions on association matters.

Article VI

Externally, the association is legally represented by the council chairperson and the association's attorney in combination. In the case of purchase, disposal, or mortgage of property, the association is represented by all members such that the members authorize Barrister (attorney) J. Valentin on their behalf to submit a purchase offer or negiotiate with Birkerød County.

Article VII

The association will as soon as possible unanimously decide on the more explicit procedures which will be valid for the association's decisions —hereafter amendments to the bylaws and the association's dissolution.

Article VIII

The present bylaws are the foundation for the association's acquisition of a building site and the elaboration of the development program, and are, therefore, of provisional character.

At the time of a final agreement on the development program the members of the association are obligated to replace the present bylaws with new association bylaws or partnership contract which secures the association a reasonable economic basis to:

- contract with the project's consultants
- contract with contractors for site preparation and construction
- prepare all public documents such as the plot plan, owner's association bylaws, contracts for water, electrical and gas services, etc.

The above mentioned economic foundation provides that the members individually or jointly obtain sufficient credit.

Article IX

If the present bylaws must be annulled, a copy certified by the association's attorney is regarded as evidence in part for the bylaws contents and in part for the share which according to the bylaws is due to all the members.

Such are the articles at the founding association meeting.

Birkerød, December 6, 1978

SELECTED BIBLIOGRAPHY

Andersen, Hans S. "Danish Low-rise Housing Cooperatives (bofællesskaber) as an Example of a Local Community Organization." *Scandinavian Housing and Planning Research* (May 1985): 49–66.

Andersen, Hans S., and Lyager, Paul. "Tæt-Lave Bofælleskaber—erfaringer, problemer, og perspektiver" (High density, Low-rise Cohousing —experiences, problems, and perspectives). *Arkitekten* (April 1984): 78–81.

Andersen, Hans S., and Nielsen, John. "Økonomisk risiko og hårdt arbejde ved bofælleskabsprojekten." (Economic risk and hard work with cohousing projects). *Blød By 13* (1981): 22—24.

Arkitektur 6 (October 1984) Entire issue is devoted to discussion of cohousing.

Bellah, Robert., et al. *Habits of the Heart: Individualism and Commitment in American Life.* New York: Harper & Row, 1985.

Bjerre, Poul, and Kløvedal Reich, Ebbe. "Fællesskabets politiske perspektiven" (The community's political perspectives). *Information*, 29 February 1984.

Bjerre, Poul, and Kløvedal Reich, Ebbe. "Fælleskabets Ubrugte Kraften" (The community's unused strengths). *Information*, 28 February 1984.

Bundgaard, Aase; Gehl, Jan; and Skoven, Erik. "Bløde Kanter" (Soft Edges). *Arkitekten* 21, (1982) 421–438.

Byggeriets Udviklingsgråd (The Building Development Council). *Veje til Bofællesskab (Way to Cohousing).* Copenhagen: 1983.

Byggeriets Udviklingsgråd. *Bofællesskabet Sol og Vind.* Copenhagen: 1982.

Byggeriets Udviklingsgråd. *Boliger og boformer i informations-samfundet (Housing and Living Forms in the Information Society).* Copenhagen: 1984.

Cronberg, Tarja, and Jantzen, Erik. *Building for People: The Theory in Practice.* Hørsholm: Statens Byggeforskningsinstitut (The Danish Building Research Institute), Report 299.

Danish National Agency for Physical Planning, Danish Ministry of Housing. *The Human Settlements Situation and Related Trends and Policies.* Publication no. 57, 1982.

"Danmarks tæt, lav bofællesskaber" *Bløde By 13* (1981): 11–15.

"Danmarks tæt, lav bofællesskaber" *Bløde By 31* (October 1984): 2326.

Davis, Sam. *The Form of Housing.* New York: Van Nostrand Reinhold, 1977.

"De blå gaden er overdækket med glass" (on Jystrup Savværket). *BoBedre* (March 1985).

Drevet, Ove R., ed. *Herfra Hvor Vi Bor (Here Where We Live).* Copenhagen: Skippershoved, 1986.

Drevet, Ove R. *Overdrevet, Et Bofælleskab.* Copenhagen: Skippershoved, 1981.

"Et godt jyske fællesskab" (on Mejdal I). *BoBedre* (October 1980): 26–35.

Fromm, Dorit. "Living-together Housing" *The Architectural Review* (April 1985): 63–71.

Gehl, Jan. *Life Between Buildings.* New York: Van Nostrand Reinhold, 1987.

Goss, Kathy, and Madsen, Per. "Shared Lives, Shared Energy." *Solar Age* (July 1982): 1619.

*Graae, Bodil. "Børn skal have Hundrede Forældre" (Children should have One Hundred Parents). *Politiken* (April 1967).

*Gudmand-Høyer, Jan. "Det manglende led mellem utopi og det forældede en familiehus" (The missing link between utopia and the dated single family house). *Information*, 26 June 1968.

*Gudmand-Høyer, Jan. "Ikke kun huse for folk-også huse af folk" (Not only houses for people--also houses by people). *Information*, 4 April 1984.

Hayden, Dolores. *Redesigning the American Dream: The Future of Housing, Work, and Family Life.* New York: W.W. Norton & Co., 1984.

"It Takes Action to Get Things Done." *Living Architecture* 1 (1983): 106–112.

Jernstøberiet, Roskilde. "Sådan gik 20 familier" (on Jernstøberiet). *BoBedre* (February 1982): 49–53.

Johnson, Michael S. "Apropos Trudeslund." *Arkitektur* (June 1982): 248.

Marcus, Clare Cooper, and Sarkissian, Wendy. *Housing as if People Mattered.* Berkeley: University of California Press, 1986.

Ministry of Housing. *Financing of Housing in Denmark. Copenhagen: 1984.*

Staten Byggeforskningsinstitut. *Tæt Lav-en boligform Idekonkurrence om byggesytemer og bebuggelsessystemer.* Report 82. Copenhagen: 1972.

"Sættedammen." *Byplan* 156. Copenhagen: 1975.

Toffler, Alvin. *The Third Wave.* New York: Bantam Books, 1980.

"Trudeslund, bofælleskab i Birkerød." *Arkitektur* (June 1982): 240–246.

"Works by Vandkunsten." *Arkitektur* 5-6. (October 1985): 196–257.

denotes newspaper articles

INDEX